My WALK *with* GOD *and* BEYOND

BOGGA

ISBN 979-8-88751-181-8 (paperback)
ISBN 979-8-88751-182-5 (digital)

Christian Faith Publishing
832 Park Avenue
Meadville, PA 16335
www.christianfaithpublishing.com

Printed in the United States of America

I have always had Jesus in my life. I can't remember when he wasn't there. I was brought up in a Greek Catholic household, and we always went to church on Sunday. That is, my mother, brother, and I. Dad just drove us there and picked us up. My mother was a devout believer and had even gone to school at church and learned how to read in Ukraine. My grandfather was very connected to the church, but I don't know how. It's kind of like when you're a kid, you skip family information. I wish I had listened more. There is no one alive now who would know the answer.

I can remember being in church and probably fidgety. My mother let me stand against the wall. I was maybe four or five. I just thought I was a big deal watching everyone and had a much better view of the priest and what he was doing.

I made my First Holy Communion at age seven. Being Greek Catholic, we were confirmed and baptized at the same time, unlike the Roman Catholics who had to perform both. In high school, all the kids were moaning that they had to attend classes for confirmation. Why didn't I?

For First Holy Communion classes, the nuns handed out a little book which I still have called *Jesus and I*. Inside it explained who God is and had many prayers, questions, and answers. I read that often and was drawn to reading it. Jesus was a very important part of my life. Some things that we were taught then were wrong, like don't bother God about the small stuff, only big important things, which is very wrong. The Bible says to pray constantly and seek Jesus out. He wants to have a relationship with us, not be a needed pitstop when you're desperate.

I took the Ten Commandments very seriously. One thing I didn't want to do was make God mad or be disappointed in me. In my book, the fourth commandment was "Honor thy Father and Mother." Respect for them was very important to me. My father also taught that quickly to us when we'd get him mad and he'd start to unbuckle his belt. This meant he intended to use it on our butts. I always respected my parents and helped them to the end of their lives. They were a fine example too. I never saw my parents argue or fight. My father respected my mother, and she him. There was no "boss." They always talked things out.

As I started first grade, I was a whiz with memorizing reading words. It worked great for second grade too. However, third grade became a problem when they came out with phonics. To me, all the words sounded the same. I could not read many words as I couldn't sound them out. This became a problem through high school. When a counselor came from high school in the seventh grade, asking what I wanted to do in life so they could set up my high school classes, I said I wanted to be a nurse. Because of my reading level problems, I was told I couldn't do college prep courses as they would involve too much reading. So I got business courses. I felt bad and stupid. I even got reading as an elective instead of art or home economics.

When I was twelve, I started to babysit. I got a big fifty cents an hour. I really enjoyed watching kids. By the time I was fifteen, I said out loud, "Someday I want to be a mother, too, and if I can't have any children, I'll adopt one." Watch what you say aloud as God is listening, and he might just give you what you ask for. Life and death are in the tongue.

At eighteen, I fell in love with a boy from high school. I was over at my girlfriend's house, hanging out, and he lived across the street. He started hanging out too. At first, I didn't care for him. He was quite handsome, and I thought maybe he was stuck up. We all went to my girlfriend's church for a night out of roller skating. Well, we started skating, and before we knew it, we were skating together. The following weekend, we did a scavenger hunt in Asbury Park, New Jersey. He gave me a muscle shell from the beach, which I still have, and put it on a necklace.

I was so head over heels in love with him. We saw each other almost every day and talked on the phone. I was a senior in high school, and he was a sophomore. He was only a year younger than me but started school later when he came from Germany. He had to go to kindergarten to learn English. Well, we were the big gossip in school as I had asked him to the senior ball, and he was only a sophomore. Lots of girls wanted him for themselves because he was so sweet and handsome. I was thrilled I was his girlfriend. I would go to church on Sunday and pray that this would work out and that someday we'd marry. I prayed that a lot.

After I graduated from high school, I decided to go to a hairdresser's school in Asbury Park. I went to Wilfred Beauty Academy in September of 1965. Danny DeVito was in the class ahead of me. I didn't get to talk with him, only his teacher was complaining he was always missing class because he went to NYC to try out for acting.

My boyfriend and I would go to the boardwalk in Asbury Park every summer. We'd also go swimming to ride the waves. One Labor Day Weekend, we went to the beach. Back then, there was no such thing as a riptide problem. This day, there was a hurricane down in Florida. We were not cautioned about going in the water. There were lots of us swimming and riding the waves. The only problem was the waves were very high, about maybe ten feet. It was great jumping over them or riding them in. However, there was a drop in the sand, and the water was deeper, and we didn't expect it to be over our heads. The waves came so quickly that I didn't have time to recover, and there was another one right away. I got really tired fast and wanted to get out.

I told my boyfriend I wanted to get out. I kept swimming to the shore but went nowhere. Finally, I got so exhausted I was just going to give up. A peace came over me, and I just stopped swimming. I was too tired. Just then, my boyfriend pulled me out of the water. He was very fit and had the strength to get me out. When I got to the blanket, I was dizzy, coughing, and sick to my stomach. It was horrible. The feeling lasted for what seemed like an eternity. I told him it would have been easier to die than live at that point. The peace I felt was just unreal.

My boyfriend and I stayed together, and when he was nineteen, he was drafted into the army in January 1968. I was devastated as I was used to seeing him all the time, and then nothing until boot camp was over. They were not allowed any visitors until the eight weeks were over. He was stationed in Fort Dix, New Jersey. There were no gates at the time, so I would pick him up on Friday night and bring him back on Sunday. That didn't last long, and he was transferred to Fort Gordon, Georgia.

He got to come home on leave in May 1968 and proposed marriage. Of course, I accepted happily. Then two weeks later, he got his orders to go to Vietnam. Now I had to decide. Did I want to get married before he left or after he came home? Thinking my parents wouldn't be happy with me going to Hawaii to see him on R & R, I had better marry him before. So we planned the wedding in two weeks, and we were married.

At the time, my mother and I were going to a Roman Catholic Church for ten years, and they refused to marry us in their church. I was able to arrange for us to get married on a Wednesday in the Greek Catholic Church fifty miles away. This was the same church my parents got married in and where my brother and I were baptized/confirmed and made our First Holy Communion. I wasn't going to let anything stop me from getting married in church.

Two weeks after our wedding, he left for Vietnam. I was sad but just kept on praying for him to be safe. I was a hairdresser at the time, and every time I thought about him being there, I'd say a prayer. My boss didn't want me to discuss it at all. I'd have to be professional about it.

I was late with my time of the month and was wondering if I was pregnant. I was bloated and seemed to be getting bigger. My girlfriend's mother was a phlebotomist but was on vacation, so someone else did my blood test to see if I was pregnant. The test came out slightly positive. That's crazy! I'd never heard of that! I was excited at the prospect of being pregnant. I wrote my husband that I thought I might be pregnant and that I might not be able to meet him in Hawaii as I'd be too close to delivery.

When her mother came back from vacation, she did my blood work again. She said there was no such thing as slightly pregnant. The test was negative. I wasn't pregnant. I was sad at the thought. I was then thinking it was a false pregnancy. My husband was confused as I was on the pill when we got married and stopped when he left. I thought, *Well, it would have screwed up our plans of building our house when he got back.*

Around the time of the Tet Offensive, January 30, 1969, I had two exact nightmares that his coffin was in the bathtub and that I wouldn't go in there. I woke my mother up and slept with her. I was scared and prayed and prayed for God to watch over him and keep him safe. God kept him safe. We joined each other on his birthday in March in Hawaii for R & R. I was so excited. All the wives waited at the base for them to come in. We found each other and hugged and kissed.

When we got back to the hotel, he was different. He was solemn and very strained and drained. This man was not my husband. We went to the beach, which was across the street. I rented a car, and we toured the island. He wanted nothing to do with driving. He was emotionally spent. We saw the North Beach where they surf and sugarcane grows in the fields. I wanted to buy some land there. He didn't want me to be stuck with it if he passed. Now you can't buy land there. Only lease it out! The week went fast, and home I went, him back to Nam.

He was offered an early out of the army if he stayed there an extra thirty days instead of coming home. He chose that and came home in August. My brother took me to the airport in Newark as he had landed at Kennedy Airport and took a taxi to Newark. The taxi driver harassed him on the drive over, telling him he went there for nothing and that it was a senseless war. By the time he got to Newark, he was very angry—not the homecoming meeting I had hoped for him.

He stayed home only for two weeks and got a job with his old boss and went to work. He told me he wanted to forget all about it and get on with our lives. He'd never talk about it, yet there was something gloomy about him. He just wasn't the same.

We got our own apartment and started our married life. I thought to myself, *Is this going to work out?* But being the good Catholic girl, yep, I would overcome this, and we'd be fine.

We started saving to build our house. I had found a model ranch house, and we got our friend to draft the plans. We were hoping to get pregnant, but nothing was happening except disappointment. My friends were having babies. Why wasn't I? While we were building our house, I begged him to apply for adoption with me. I wanted to be a mother. After my begging and pleading, he agreed, and we applied for adoption. We were told there was a five-year wait for an infant. I didn't care. That was hope to me!

We started out clearing the land and got it bulldozed. He got a transit and set up the stakes for the footing. We dug out the footing so it could get poured after putting the reinforcing rods in. My arm started hurting from the digging. I went to a doctor who said I had tennis elbow from the repetitive motion of being a hairdresser and digging. It was all too much for my arm. I got painkillers and had to use them just to be able to work. I could hardly hold a comb in my hand.

We got the foundation poured with the help of his boss's brother. It was such a big area for just him to do it. I tried to help, too, but the men did that job. It was too much for my arm. We started the foundation. The cement blocks were too heavy for me to lift. But I was able to lay some flat cement blocks pretty well. After the first day, we laid only twelve blocks. My father-in-law helped the next day and laid fifty blocks. This was ridiculous.

A patron at work, her husband was a mason. We contacted him, and he laid the rest of the foundation. He did it in a day. God only knows how long it would have taken us to do that. I had to talk my husband into letting him do it. It would waste too much time and energy. We let the foundation rest for the winter.

In April 1971, my father had a stroke and was paralyzed on the left side. There was nothing they could do for him. It was a permanent condition. My mother faithfully took care of him. His job tried to not pay the insurance that helped pay the mortgage. Every month, someone would come to the house to see if he improved. He didn't.

Eventually, his doctor had to sign a statement every month, stating it was a permanent condition and he wouldn't recover.

My husband's father passed before we finished the house. Pop was the nicest easygoing man, and we missed him dearly.

We started it in the spring again. He framed it out with a friend. When it was 105 degrees, we started the roof rafters. He said, "If you can just hold up the beam for me, I can get started."

I was scared of heights. I prayed for God to give me strength as I was really scared. I did it. It was crazy and really hot, but he started it. The man was really determined to get it done. We got it framed and sheeted on the money we had saved. We didn't do anything but work hard. We applied for a construction loan then. We had to have that much done to get the loan. It was for twenty years. We then completed the house. From start to finish, it took two years.

My husband was so proud of himself. You'd think he did it all by himself. I was there, being his helper four days a week, and worked the other three. It was teamwork, bud!

In the meantime, we went to an infertility doctor to see what the problem was. The tests for me were really painful, but I grinned and bore them. It seemed that I had endometriosis and had to have surgery or face a hysterectomy by the time I was thirty-two. Even after surgery, we only had a 10 percent chance of me getting pregnant. I still kept praying for either one.

We moved into our house after two years of building it. It was wonderful. I then had my surgery and was laid up for six weeks. However, I felt like a new woman. I felt energic and very different. I was told not to vacuum for six weeks so I could heal. So I didn't vacuum. My husband said I was babying myself too much, just doing doctor's orders. I wanted to hang up drapes and pictures and asked him to do it. He told me he didn't want to put any holes in the walls. I had to nag him to eventually get that done. I quit working in the beauty salon as there was no future for me in it. There was no sick leave, no vacation pay, and if you didn't go to work, you didn't get paid. I wanted a Monday through Friday job with some kind of benefits.

My neighbor across the street worked in a dental lab. He said they were hiring for a secretarial position and suggested I apply. I got the job as I had the experience in high school for it, including bookkeeping. Before I accepted the job, there was the condition that if I needed to go to the doctor up north, I could take off when scheduled. They agreed.

The neighbor and I went to work together, carpooling. I enjoyed the job and made some nice friends. Once in a while, the crew would go out for drinks, and I'd go. My husband wasn't crazy about the idea as all he wanted to do was stay at home. He didn't want to socialize at all. I stayed at that job for two years. After a while, I became office manager. It was a hectic job doing the office work, checking in the dentures and bridges that came in, calling dentists to pay their bills, and doing inventory. They hired a helper for me. I taught her the job. The office was so hectic I kept track that I was interrupted every sixty to ninety seconds, either by phone calls or the employee needing something. I was burned out from this job. Things got slow, and they wanted to do a layoff. The other girl needed the money to support her family. The boss hated to lay her off. I said, "Then lay me off, not her."

I had made friends with a couple that worked there, and we went to their house for dinner. We saw each other frequently, and the husband did some photography and took some nice pictures of us. When we'd go over to their house, we'd talk about God a lot. Eventually, I'd go to church with them. Hubby didn't want to have anything to do with that, no matter how we tried to talk him into it.

I decided to become a home health aide for a while. I wanted to help people in some way. I got certified and went to work. I enjoyed being able to go to people's houses and help them. I'd give them showers and food and do some cleaning too. One day, I was cleaning, and the TV had the *700 Club* on. The lady had gone to bed, and as I had been dusting, they started praying for people. I decided to join in the prayer. He said to touch the place where you need to be healed. Figuring to heal my uterus, I put my hands on my abdomen. As they prayed, I felt warmth go through my abdomen. Wow, God had done something for sure.

In the fall of 1976, I decided to take two courses in college to change my career. I figured taking two classes would show me if I could do it or not. I took Accounting I and Introduction to Business Administration. Surprisingly, I got an A in both. In January of '77, I took Accounting II and got a B. So I wasn't stupid after all. I could do it if I applied myself.

On New Year's Eve, 1976, we got a letter from the New Jersey Division of Youth & Family Services. They asked if we were still interested in adoption. I was so excited! My prayers were going to be answered. Thank you, God! We did all the paperwork and home inspections and just waited. It seemed like an eternity waiting to hear from them. But I'd waited this long. What was a few more months later? I still wasn't getting pregnant.

In May of 1977, our friends asked me if I wanted to go to a charismatic prayer meeting at their church. They had been going and said that it was great and that people spoke in tongues and prophesized. I was all for it. It was very strange at first to be in this environment, but I did enjoy it. The next week, I went back again. While the praying was going on, I felt very peaceful and calm. I had my eyes closed, and there appeared Jesus. He had his garment on and long hair and a beard. There was no mistake it was Jesus. I was so excited beyond belief. I couldn't wait to tell my friends. Wow, I had seen Jesus!

The next week at the prayer meeting, as I sat there, all of a sudden, I started speaking in tongues. I was uttering words that I hadn't heard before. It was strange but comforting. There were two words I did know, and they were *Jesus* in Ukrainian, and I'd say "my heart" (pronounced a bit differently). Others I said were to seek Jesus with my heart, nothing anyone would recognize. I just couldn't believe the Holy Spirit had given me this gift. I still do speak in tongues today. It's like my soul talking to God for me the words I can't express.

The next week, at the prayer meeting, I was joining in by speaking in tongues and listening to everyone else, and I saw a vision of a little girl. These visions were quick and didn't last very long, but I can still picture them in my mind. Wow, this little girl was so cute and tiny. I couldn't wait to tell my husband. By this time, he was kind of believing all the things that had happened to me at the prayer meetings. Our friends were very excited at all of this happening to me. So now I was waiting to hear about the baby from DYFS.

In the meantime, my husband's truck battery died. He was mad. I said, "Why don't you put your hands on the hood of the truck and ask God to start the truck?" He looked at me. "He'll start it," I said.

Skeptically, he put his hands on the hood and told God if he kept the truck running, he would go to church every Sunday. I then turned the key, and it started! But when he didn't keep his word and go to church, he had to go buy a new battery.

A few weeks later, I got a phone call saying that they had a baby girl for us, about nine months old. I was the only Ukraine Catholic in the state on the application. They wanted us to come and see her. If we wanted her, we could bring her home. I told my husband. He was so excited. However, I told him that the baby that I saw in my vision was not nine months old. She was an infant. Something was wrong. But we went to see her. We spent time with her and got her information. She was a beautiful blonde-haired, blue-eyed girl. She'd fit in our family well. However, her history was that she was conceived in a mental institution, and both parents were schizophrenic. They left us alone to talk.

I told my husband I didn't know much about schizophrenia, but it was not anything we wanted to deal with. He wanted to take her home. I said, "*No*. That's not the baby I saw at the prayer meeting. We're not taking her."

On our paperwork, one thing we wouldn't accept was mental illness in the history. They told us if we changed our minds to let them know. I went to the library and investigated it. We were both very deflated about this, but I was sticking to my belief. No!

In Mid-July, we got another call from DYFS saying they had a baby girl for us. She was Irish Catholic, and they wanted her to be raised Catholic, so they selected us. She fit all our criteria and was five weeks old. I told my husband, "This has to be the one." We got all the stuff ready for her homecoming. We got the call on a Monday and went there on a Friday. As soon as I saw her, I told my husband that this was the baby that I saw in the vision. "We can take her home." We were so excited.

Back then, there were no car seats. I had to borrow a plastic carrier from a girlfriend to bring her home in. I sat in the back seat, holding her to be safe. Finally, I was a mother! They sent us home with some diapers and formula. I was instructed to feed her every two hours. We got home by noon.

A few people came to see her. The neighbor from across the street came and said that the baby was following me with her eyes as I walked into the bedroom. She just kept her eyes on me. I said, "She's noticing a mother for a change." She had been in foster care for almost five weeks.

What I noticed was that she was going to the side to get her bottle. I figured that the bottle had been propped up and the woman had other kids to care for and this baby was last on the list. I held her close each time and fed her. By evening, the baby was still crying, and so was I. I didn't know what to do. So I called a girlfriend down the street, and she came over with rice cereal. She fed her a couple of spoonsful, and she stopped crying. She was just hungry.

That first week was a big adjustment for me as I had never cared for a baby 24/7. By the following Sunday, I was ready for church by myself. My husband said, "Hold on, you're not going to church! This is what you wanted. Stay home and watch the baby."

I wasn't able to go to church for quite a long time after that. I was thinking he was afraid, but for an hour? The baby developed colic and only slept fifteen minutes a day. The rest of the time, I had to entertain her. I got her some meds for the colic, and it finally subsided. At three months, she had three teeth, at six months, six teeth, and so on.

At two months old, I repeated the vowel sounds numerous times a day. At three months old, she said, "UUU."

I looked at her, thinking, *OMG, this kid just recited a vowel sound to me.*

At seven months, she said, "All gone." The doctor was shocked at this age, repeating two-syllable words. I kept a log of everyday occurrences. It was just amazing. At one year old, she was saying five-syllable words. Her vocabulary was amazing. The more words I threw at her, the more she picked up and repeated them in the appropriate context. My mother was watching her at a year and a half old one day. They were talking to her neighbor, and my mother said, "Let's go change your diaper."

My daughter said, "Don't worry, Grandma, my diaper will absorb my peepee." My mother's neighbor never forgot that. She was just amazed.

My husband at the time was enjoying her but came home moody. I had to have dinner ready when he got home and put her to bed on time to have time for him after he slept on the couch while I cleaned up from dinner. He didn't even take his plate to the sink. I was told the inside of the house was my responsibility and the outside was his. He had his garden, and I had to blanch the vegetables at night after dinner. If I took a shower, he'd bring her with him to see what Mommy was doing. Not a moment of peace. After all, this is what I wanted, and he did it for me.

When she was age two, I decided it was time to get a job and go to work in the evenings. I got a job at McDonald's, which was opening in Lakehurst. I was there on opening day. What a relief it was to be with adults. I worked Monday, Tuesday, Thursday, and Friday. She cried for me, and he brought her one day when I was working the drive-thru. To this day, she remembers me giving her an ice cream cone in the drive-thru. It was exciting for her.

My mother would watch her if I got a call asking if I could do lunch hour if someone called out. I'd drive her to my parents' house, and he'd pick her up on the way back. Every paycheck, I had to pay for the new car that I had to get due to exhaust fumes coming in the other one. The more time went on, the more distant we became. He wouldn't talk about Vietnam and would be distant, angry, and moody. We'd argue our differences out all the time. There wasn't a name for it then, but he had PTSD for sure.

By the third year of her life, he said, "When are you going to get a real job to help me out?" Really, I brought home real money. I worked until 1:00 a.m. and had to be up at 6:00 a.m. to make his breakfast and lunch. I tried to go back to sleep before my girl woke up. I was exhausted. Since this job was my idea, I got no mercy. We grew further apart. I prayed for financial security for myself.

When our daughter was three and a half, she got strep throat three weeks in a row. I would sleep with her in another bedroom so I could keep track of her temperature. Her fever would spike at night. Meanwhile, I was still working at McDonald's four days a week. I was exhausted. I hadn't slept with my husband in three weeks. One morning, he woke me up at 5:00 a.m. and said, "Come on, I gotta have it." He'd preach to me how a wife is supposed to submit to her husband.

As I walked to our bedroom, exhausted from going to bed at 1:00 a.m., I looked up to God and said, "I'm doing this for you, not for him!"

About two weeks later, I rolled over in bed and felt sick to my stomach and wanted to heave. Nothing came out, but the sickness was there. Morning through evening, the same thing occurred. I was either sick and dying or pregnant! Sure enough, after nine years of trying, then giving up, yep, I was pregnant. The infertility doctor said if I should get pregnant to be careful as I could possibly miscarry easily. Again, working at McDonald's was hard work being on my feet, especially having sink duty and lifting heavy things to clean. I started to get back pains. I told my boss, and he laid me off.

The first three months of pregnancy were bad with me feeling nauseous all day. I had to force myself to eat for the baby's sake. The next three months were great. I felt pretty good. I still took it easy for which my husband said, "Well, you're not the first woman to have a baby, what's your problem?" Really, how would he know how I felt?

On March 31, 1981, my dad passed away from a heart attack. I kept calm for the baby's sake. I had told my daughter that Mommy was going to have a baby. That babies come out of Mommy's tummy. She asked if she came out of my belly. I said no, another mommy's belly. I wanted her to know at an early age that she was adopted just in case someone else told her before me. After all, the whole neighborhood knew. It was no secret.

One day, lying in bed, I said to God, "You let me know what my daughter looked like before we got her. Can you show me what I'm having now?" Sure enough, I had a vision of a little girl in a blue dress. I actually have a picture on display of her in that dress at age two.

When it was close to the time of delivery, my doctor said the baby was breech and that if it didn't turn around before delivery, I'd have to have a C-section. Well, that wasn't what I wanted. Again, I went to God and said, "If I forgive my father for something he did when I was young, would you turn the baby in the right position for birth?" Sure enough, the baby was turned at the next visit.

At 7:30 one July morning, I started labor. My husband went to work, and my best friend took me to the doctor's office for a check-up. Sure enough, I was in labor. I called my husband at work, and he came home. The doctor said, "Come to the hospital when you can't stand the pains anymore."

We counted the contractions all day. Being it was the first delivery and I was thirty-four, it was going to be a long haul. By that evening, we went to the hospital. My husband was with me all the time, trying to divert my attention from the labor pains and helping me to breathe as we learned in classes. He rubbed my back to ease the pain. Finally, this was the first time I ever saw my husband show compassion for me. He felt so bad to see me in such pain.

At midnight, I got a shot to bring on labor faster. Well, it was harder, but it wasn't faster. At 2:00 a.m., the doctor said, "Stop pushing, you're not far enough along to deliver." So for two hours, I couldn't push. It was like impossible not to, but I knew I could hurt the baby if I did. Then by 4:00 a.m., the doctor said I could push. Forty minutes later, I was rolled into the delivery room, pushing and pushing but getting nowhere.

At 5:00 a.m., the doctor came in and said, "If you don't deliver in five minutes, I'll give you an epidural shot." I didn't want that because at that point in time, I'd have to lie flat on my back for eight hours or get headaches. My girlfriend had headaches for years after that shot. No way was I having that. I didn't go through all this labor with nothing, to then get an epidural shot.

I said to God, "Please do something now. I don't want a shot after all of this."

The nurse got on a step stool and said to me, "Let me know when you have another contraction."

I did, and she took her arm and pushed on my belly, and out popped the baby's head. "Thank you, Lord!" My husband had to sit down. He looked like he was going to pass out.

My older daughter thought it was great to have a sister. She held her on her lap when we got home. She was also Mommy's little helper. I breastfed the baby for three months. My husband was wonderful then. He came home and had to cook dinner at times, did the dishes, and cleaned up while I fed the baby. As soon as I stopped breastfeeding her, the party was over. Back to the same old routine. Plus, I had to go to work and help out again and come home to the mess on the table that I had left to go to work. He cleaned up nothing, not even teaching the older daughter how to load the dishwasher.

My generation was supposed to be able to stay home and be a mother only. Economically, things changed, and I had to work to make ends meet.

One morning, I woke up, and the baby was coughing, a croup cough. *Okay, now what do I do? Take her to the ER myself or call an ambulance?* What if she needed oxygen? I called 911. The EMTs came right away and saw my kitchen mess. I was mortified. I apologized that I worked till 1:00 a.m., and my husband left it for me.

They said, "Don't worry about that, we've seen much worse." My first and last trip, hopefully, to the hospital.

My oldest daughter said, "Wow, Mommy, they drove really fast!" My baby was in a croup tent for a few days and did well on the meds and came home.

After I had the baby, I didn't really lose weight, even though I had only gained twenty-seven pounds. I was very frustrated with my husband, and to calm myself from the arguing, I'd comfort eat. I gained another ten pounds. He'd nagged me about that a lot. The more he complained about things, the more I ate. He was always trying to control me in some way. One day, he came home and said to me, "You're a fat slob. Nobody else would want you, and you're lucky I'm supporting your fat ass."

I was speechless and just stared at him. I decided I couldn't deal with these mood swings and arguing much longer. I prayed to God to please help him and change him. I also prayed for financial security again. I didn't want to depend on a man to support me.

My sister-in-law's father passed. We went to the funeral home. We were all downstairs talking before going to the church. A discussion came up about my father. My brother had anxiety when he talked about our father because of how he treated him. He was always riding him. He had gotten him a job after the navy in a factory of the same name as him. My brother hated it and quit. My father told him he was never going to amount to anything. For the rest of his life, he tried proving to our father he was wrong.

Anyway, we went to church for the Mass as they were Catholic. During the Mass, I was thinking about the conversation we had about our father. Then I heard my father say to me, "Don't think of me then, think of me later." It brought up a bad memory of him, and I had uncontrollable crying. People were looking at me as to why I was crying so much about her father. But it was about my father that I was crying. I was just pouring out the sorrow from my memory of abuse from being a baby. No one would believe. I must have been only about a year and a half old. He was changing my diaper. I felt the pain and screamed out, and then he gave me a bottle. It's just as vivid now as it was that day in my mind now. The pain is healed now, but I'll never forget it.

I was in church one Sunday and was praying about something and asking God if I should go a certain way. I needed guidance. In church, I looked up at the wall and saw the devil smiling at me. I couldn't believe my eyes—the devil in church! When God wants to tell you something, it doesn't matter where you are. He'll answer you!

Once again, my husband complained about when I was going to get a real job and help him out. So in 1988, I went out to get a real job. I got an assistant manager's job at Fashion Bug. The hours were rough on the family. I had to work five days a week, with three of them nights, every Saturday and every other Sunday. By now, the kids were eight and twelve, so the older one could watch the younger one. If I worked late, he'd have to cook dinner. I hated working on Saturday as the family was together, and I couldn't be there. This didn't make for a happy married life at all.

Finally, in May 1989, he came home from work and wanted to have fun. I was exhausted from working five days a week, and I didn't want to do anything. He said he couldn't live like this anymore and wanted to get his own place. I said, "Fine, if that's what you want to do."

A friend of his from work was telling him of the women he'd have every weekend, each week a different one. This must have seemed exciting to him as we had married young, twenty and twenty-one. The grass looked greener on the other side of the street, I guess. So at the end of the month, when we came home from being out, all his things were gone. It was kind of creepy, but the pressure was off. No more arguing or fighting.

He didn't mention where he'd gone, and the girls were worried. It was Memorial Day, and he didn't come home nor call for the girls. They were sad and worried. We got in the car and drove from one apartment complex to another, looking for his van, but we couldn't find him. We never looked at the townhouses his boss owned, but that's where he went.

I saw a lawyer. She said to write in a notepad everything about my marriage. So that's what I did. Sixty handwritten pages later, I was done. She filed for divorce. He wanted to give me $75 a week for support. Yeah, what was that going to do? Well, the judge decided on $230 a week and was told to get another job if he couldn't live on his pay.

And so it began, living without him. At first, it was sad, but not arguing anymore was great. We had peace and quiet. He got the girls every other weekend, and on the off week, Thursday. One time, the hot water heater flame went out. I called to tell him to come light the flame so we could shower. He said, "You wanted your freedom, take care of it yourself."

I said, "The girls need to take a shower."

He refused to come and turn the pilot light on. The next day, I went down to the propane gas company, saw the kind of hot water heater we had, and asked the guy how to light the pilot light. He showed me how, and I came home and lit it! I felt triumphant that I could do it. He called and said he could come and light it today. I told him, "Not necessary, I did it myself" (*The Little Red Hen*, my favorite Golden Book).

The electric dryer stopped drying the clothes. We had a book on the dryer. I went to the appliance parts place and got a new thermostat for it. Step by step, I followed the directions and fixed it. In high school, I scored highest in mechanical ability. Well, it certainly paid off. My girls were proud and impressed because nothing was going to stop me.

I didn't want to depend on another man again. Before we adopted our daughter, I wanted to go to college for accounting. He didn't want me to go because I could get attacked in the parking lot. Well, I went anyway. I was able to complete three classes only as we adopted the baby. I had a hard time in school with reading. Phonics was my issue. Everything sounded the same, so they didn't want me to take college prep in high school as they didn't think I could keep up with the reading. I wanted to be a nurse then, and that ended that. I was determined to raise my girls to be independent and to get a good education so they didn't have to rely on a man to support them!

My mother and I went to a Halloween party at a local First Aid Squad. We had a blast dancing. This was my first outing since he left. He always wanted to stay home or visit my girlfriend and her family or occasionally go to a movie, but no other fun. At the dance, I met a single woman who loved the dance also. It was her first time out too. She lived in the same neighborhood as my ex came from. Ironically, she was the daughter of his first boss in the construction field.

We hit it off and decided to meet at a singles dance. At that time, there was always a singles dance every night of the week. I joined Parents Without Partners too.

I met other women at the dances and became friends with them. I was out most nights, dancing. The oldest daughter was old enough to babysit, so I was free to get out and have fun. I was having so much fun but didn't realize the toll it took out on my daughters with Mom being out most nights. I figured they had to go to sleep anyway. What was the difference? I was free as a bird to do what I wanted and not under anybody's control anymore.

I did learn later that it was very hard on them. I was only thinking of myself and trying to find out who I was then. They weren't neglected. I had always made sure the dinners were organized and left instructions on how to cook something as a lot of the nights, I had to work late. I closed the store at 9:00 p.m., then went to a dance. They had to go to bed then, so all was okay then, right?

New Year's Eve that year, my ex had to do an oil change on my car as required by law. He started to come on to me in the garage. Wow, it had been a long time since I was even kissed. After he left, did I make a mistake about this divorce thing? Maybe we could date and fall in love again. After the dance, I stopped at his apartment. He wasn't home. I waited in my car for him to come home. It got so late I went home.

The next day, I went to see him unannounced. We talked, and he showed me the apartment. Really nice place. I asked him if he wanted to maybe date. He said no. I said, "If I got down on one knee and begged you?"

He said, "No, don't do that."

I said, "Someday you'll regret this." And I left.

At the Valentine's Day dance, I met a really nice man, and we started to date. He was such a gentleman and loved to dance. We danced all night when we went to the dances. I invited him over for dinner. The girls liked him. Then my ex called me. He wanted to come home as he and his girlfriend had broken up and he was alone now. I told him no, that I found a nice man who treated me like I wanted to be treated and that he could stay at his place and I'd stay here with the girls. Really, that he still loved me and never wanted to be without me anymore? No, only because he didn't have anyone anymore.

The following Good Friday, my boyfriend came over to talk. He said he couldn't see me anymore as he was in a 12-step plan for Alcoholics Anonymous and wasn't supposed to be in any kind of relationship. We had gone to a nightclub the weekend before, and I could tell something was wrong. He was having a difficult time dealing with the atmosphere at the bar and band environment. He had played in a band and had to drink to be able to do it. It just brought up too many memories for him. He couldn't handle it. I was devasted to think it ended. He was like my ideal kind of guy, thought that was it.

I then met another guy, and we hit it off. He was from Czechoslovakia. That's where my paternal grandfather was born in a covered wagon. This had to be a sign from God. I thought that this was good. The only thing was he needed his green card to stay. He was a little too obsessed with the green card. I even talked with his lawyer about his becoming a citizen. He said if I felt up to five years that he married me to become a citizen, I could get him deported. He proposed, and we were going to be married. I had a lot at stake here. The kids liked him, but if I married, then I would be forced to sell the house we built, and the ex would get half.

On the Sunday, before we were to get married, he came over while I was working to finish painting the kitchen. My daughter said to him, "We're excited about you and Mom getting married and you living with us."

He said to her, "Well, maybe I'll move in and maybe I won't."

When I got home, my daughter told me what he said. He then called to tell me his father died in Czechoslovakia. "When a family member dies, you have to postpone the wedding."

I told him, "This is America, and we don't have those rules. But you don't have to worry about it because I'm not marrying you on Friday or any other day! Forget it." I had a lot to lose with this marriage, and God just took things in hand and changed it just in time. Thank you, Lord!

So for our honeymoon, I took the girls to the Amish Country in Lancaster, Pennsylvania. We had a wonderful time. While there, we went to President Buchanan's home in Lancaster. It was quite luxurious for its era with indoor plumbing, a bathtub, and heating. As we walked into the living room, a piano started playing music. As soon as I heard it, I said to myself, "I played that music before." I knew it. What in the world? How could that be? I never played the piano.

I looked at a picture of the woman who was his niece. He never married. She had the same hair and skin color as me. Could that have been me in another lifetime? I kind of always thought we'd come back until we fulfill what is expected, then we don't have to come back anymore. Strange.

I continued my dancing fun. I got promoted to store manager in another town. The shrink there was at 5 percent. My girlfriend from the Halloween dance was my assistant manager now. That was a little awkward at first, me having to tell her what to do. The company was offering any store manager who dropped the shrink $500. I decided to concentrate on this.

The girls watched the front door constantly, watched the dressing rooms. Where were the clothes going out the door? So I decided to check the layaway cards against the inventory in the back. Well, it didn't match. There were supposed to be more clothes back there, but there weren't. Okay, now the clothes had to be going out the back door! Only management could open the back door. I called my supervisor. Now she didn't like me from day one. Why? I don't know. I told her my theory about the missing inventory.

We decided to put more clothes on layaway. Sure enough, some were gone the next week. This was a fictitious customer layaway, so we knew it was her. The supervisor came in and had a meeting with her and fired her. I never saw my friend again.

My supervisor brought in a new assistant. I could see this was her up-and-coming manager to be someday, a real gung ho girl who wanted to be somebody, maybe take the supervisor's job someday. Another woman came into the store a lot. She wanted to be an employee in the worst way. Don't know what connections she had, but she came in under my assistant manager.

September came around, and it was slow. A lot of our clientele were Jewish, and this was their holiday. Well, my assistant said to the second assistant, "Well, this Jewish holiday is killing our business. I don't know any Jews and I don't work with any Jews."

With that, the second assistant said, "Well, I'm Jewish."

So the battle started. I was off that day. They were at each other when I wasn't around. The second assistant's husband was a manager of some big fashion store and was sick and tired of her complaining about my assistant. The supervisor made the assistant manager apologize to her. Instead of the supervisor separating them by store as she should have done, she didn't. It continued, and her husband told her she had to quit. Then he called corporate headquarters and told them he would file a complaint with the Anti-Defamation League if they didn't do something about it. They told the supervisor to get rid of the situation. I got demoted along with my assistant, and the second assistant quit. I got transferred to the supervisor's store, and my assistant went elsewhere.

I knew in my heart this wasn't good. Now I was the assistant to my supervisor, which was weird as she was hardly ever in the store. I did my job there to the best of my ability as always. The supervisor heard good things about me from the girls, such as I was always at them to work and not fool around. I made them do their job.

One day, the supervisor came in and left her keys at home by mistake. She was upset she'd have to go home and get the keys. I looked at the door and said, "You don't have to do that. I can take the door off the hinges, and it will be open."

I was her hero then. After the New Year, I got called into the office with her supervisor. I got fired because of the incident in my store. I got to make a statement as to her showing favoritism to my assistant while she was under me. I later heard that the assistant caused trouble and finally got fired.

I went home feeling so low. It wasn't my fault, yet I was being punished. Now what was I going to do? I had children to support. I couldn't be a hairdresser anymore. What would I do now? I was sad and depressed. I tried to get into the school system, but it's who you know there. I couldn't substitute teach—not enough education. "Lord, what can I do now?" Every time I'd go to the mall, I'd feel panicky to go in. Was it PTSD?

I had been a home health aide before. Maybe I should do that again. So back to class I went to get recertified again. I got put on the schedule and back to work. One of my favorite ladies was a nice Polish lady. We became good friends, and I'm still friends with her daughter that's ninety now. When I was there, I'd help her shower and give her something to eat. I'd bring my rollers and hair dryer and set her hair and comb it out. She was so happy, and we enjoyed talking. I got her and my mother to talk on the phone as they both could talk in Polish. I made other great friends with the people I worked with. I really enjoyed my job and making people laugh and be happy. I just wanted to bring some sunshine into people's lives.

On November 3, 1992, election day, I was driving to work. It was a nice day, and I carefully watched my speed limit, going through the senior development at twenty-five miles per hour. I came to an intersection, and *bam*! A car hit me on the driver's side front fender, and my car whipped around and hit hers. I was still in the intersection, and her car was on a corner lawn. I quickly thought, *Well, I feel okay.* I didn't dare move, though. *I'll wait for the EMT to come.* I looked up into the sky and said, "Really, God, what were you thinking? First, I'm separated, then a divorce, then I get fired, and now an accident! Really, Lord! All this in three years."

They carefully took me out of the car. I could walk and got in the ambulance, and there was the woman from the other car. I said, "What were you doing, arguing with your husband about who to vote for?" I was getting angry with her. They put her in another ambulance.

I went to the hospital, and they did tests. I had a herniated disc and was in a lot of pain. My chest hurt from the seat belt along with my abdomen and neck. They called my mother, and her neighbor brought her to the hospital.

A policeman came to take my statement. He said I hit her car.

I got all excited. "I hit her car?"

He said, "Relax, we're on your side, she didn't stop at the stop sign."

I got sent home with meds and painkillers. My neighbor brought us both home to my house. My car was totaled. I had just gotten that used Chevy station wagon with only twenty-five thousand miles. I was sick about that. Now what was I going to do? I couldn't go back to being an HHA. "Lord, what are you doing to me?" The pain down the leg was so bad I could hardly sit. No place was comfortable for me.

The girls were worried about me. I said, "Don't worry, I'll be okay." *God, how can I be without a job again?* I started to get vertigo with no rhyme or reason for getting it at all. I went to the chiropractor for help. I started to collect Disability Unemployment. I still was clueless about a job. The ex didn't care. He didn't even call to hear how I was. I rented a car, and it sat there for days because I was afraid to get in and drive. Since I was only working part-time then, I didn't get much pay. I got $100 a week from my car insurance and my disability check, barely making it as far as my pay. Why hadn't my insurance man advised me about covering my salary if I was in a car accident? He didn't do his best for me with that. You pay all this money and don't have the right coverage. Then the woman's husband wanted to sue me for a million dollars because he fainted in the car. Good luck on collecting that!

On my last check from the state was a statement if I wasn't able to go back to my job to file with the Division of Vocational Rehabilitation, then I had to get retrained for a job. Now why didn't they say this before? I called right away and got an appointment. I saw a counselor, filled out papers, and she made an appointment for psychological testing to see what I would be able to do as far as schooling. I got a pamphlet for a vocational school. I loved art, so I thought of drafting, but could I make a living at it? Well, I chose a medical assisting course. I went for my psych evaluation. I was really scared. I don't know why. I guess all these years had taken a toll on me. I survived the evaluation and did well on it.

I started school. It lasted six months. I learned the history of medicine, medical terminology, taking BP, and even drawing blood. Then I did three months of internship at a hospital in medical records. I liked that job, but it was temporary. It was going to end soon, and I was getting panicky again about the uncertainty of it. When I was kind of at the end of my rope, I got a call from my counselor that there was an opening in the office and I should come in for an interview. I was excited! A state job, Monday through Friday, weekends off—my dream job. I went to the interview and got hired. I had to go to the Labor Building to take a typing test. My weak point. It was only thirty words per minute, and I did fifty in school to pass. This was a one-shot deal. I did it! I was a state worker. Thank you, God!

I loved this job and gave my all to it. I even got an hour for lunch but didn't know what to do with all that time. Everyone was nice, and I tried to not get involved with office politics. I was part of the secretarial section, and then there were the counselors and management.

I joined a dating service in town and got hooked up with someone from the next town. We hit it off right away. He was really nice. We went out to eat and became fast friends. The girls liked him too. We saw each other several times a week and talked almost every day.

One October day, I came home from work, and my oldest daughter told me to sit down. She had something to tell me. My only brother and only sibling had died of a pulmonary embolism. He had had a heart attack eight years before that. He had visited with us in January and said he had a pleural thickened from his lungs being exposed to asbestos at his job. He was a plumbing supervisor. That was the last we saw him alive. Now the hardest thing I had to do was go and tell my mother.

My mother was a tiny woman at four-foot-eleven inches. She was a gentle woman who worked hard all her life, providing a nice home for us. She loved being a mother and running the home along with cooking, sewing, mowing the lawn, and changing the curtains/drapes for the seasons. She was always there for me and I for her. Now I had to tell her that her only son was gone. Her co-op apartment was a little over a mile from my house. I told her, and she broke down and cried. I made arrangements for Mom, myself, and my youngest daughter to fly to California. The oldest daughter stayed home. She was in college.

At the funeral parlor, my sister-in-law had them play songs he liked, especially "My Way." Yes, he did it his way for sure—smoked, drank, ate out all the time. Had a great personality and spent money like crazy. At the grave, we had a rose we put on his coffin before they lowered it. A song by Seal, "Kiss from a Rose," was out. I think of him every time I hear it. Mom never talked about it with me. She always kept up a good front, but I'm sure it wrecked her inside.

When my father died, I asked her, "Is it better you don't have to take care of Dad anymore or put up with him?"

She said, "At least he was a breathing human in the house instead of being alone."

I had never lived alone, so I didn't know. My dad had a stroke and was paralyzed for ten years in bed. Back then, there were no adult diapers. They had no washing machine as the water level was too high, and too much water would cause the septic tank to back up into the tub. Mom would take the clothes to the laundromat at the corner. She took her cart as she didn't drive. When we all still lived there on Saturday nights, Mom took the bath first, me second, my brother third, and my dad last—all in the same water!

I had gotten engaged to my boyfriend. My oldest daughter was graduating high school and had the rare opportunity to see the ex. It was uncomfortable seeing him with my fiancée, but it was what it was.

Life wasn't moving with us. My fiancée was fixing up his house for two years to sell and still working on it. He'd never been married. He worked at his own slow pace. We decided to get counseling. I knew the doctor from work as we'd have to type letters and case notes about the clients. I'd seen her at work. So he agreed to go. We'd been engaged for two years already. He blurted out to the counselor, "She thinks we're getting married this year, but we're not."

The counselor and I looked at each other.

We wanted to screen in our small back porch. The fiancée helped with securing the metal in the very hard cement, using a diamond-tip drill bit. Then we put up the studs. The next day, he was going to mow his lawn first, then come and help with putting up the screening. We got tired of waiting for him and started with the screening. I had learned a lot of carpentry from my ex, so we started to staple the screen. As we were screening, he came and was tired and wanted to nap on my couch. As we were working, my daughter said, "Mom, what's wrong with this picture?"

I said, "He's tired."

Well, I was tired too of him dragging his feet about getting married and working on his house. Finally, I said, "Let's take a break for a month." So we did. I'd go dancing with my girlfriends. He hated my music. I got a letter from him about how the leaves were turning and he was waiting to hear from me. He had gone to see the counselor, and she told him to write me a letter but keep it light.

Well, I called him and talked about the letter. "I'm supposed to be the love of your life, and you talk about the leaves! Not how much you love me and want me to be your wife. No. Leaves!"

That was the end of the engagement. I didn't even like his music, and he didn't like disco or my love songs. I once sent him words to the song "Have You Ever Really Loved a Woman?" Did he get this very romantic song? No. He asked very sarcastically, "Have you ever really loved a man?"

"Yes, I was married to one for twenty years." Clueless.

I told my mother, "Mom, I broke off my engagement. If you want to move in with us, it's okay."

My room was big enough for my queen bed and her full-size bed. This was a great idea at first. We agreed she'd clean and wash dishes and I'd cook. Each kid was responsible to wash their own clothes. She had macular degeneration and couldn't see very well and loved living with us for the company.

I took my mom to an Atlantic City casino to see a show starring Connie Francis. As we were waiting for the show to begin, I saw this man very attentively pushing this woman in a wheelchair. He was taking care of her every need. I said to my mom, "That's the kind of man I need—a caring, loving man."

In later January 1997, I got a phone call from my ex. The man had never talked to me in years. He asked me, "I really want to know, did you ever cheat on me when I was in Vietnam?"

"*No*, if I could have gone with you to fight, I would have. *No*, I never cheated on you." I loved this man so much it was almost idolatry. Now he must have gotten this from his sister as she once called me up, drunk, asking me if I cheated on him when he went to Vietnam. I said, "*No*, that's crazy, I never did that."

When I was a hairdresser, a coworker liked this marine stationed at a nearby base. She had to go through back roads only to get there. It was about twenty miles away. She didn't want to go alone, so I said I'd drive her. My husband was at war, and I had lots of time after work. I didn't want to sit home and worry, so I took her. My sister-in-law put this crazy idea in her head I was cheating. Her best friend was my friend's sister. Why didn't she ask them instead of assuming

I was doing something wrong? So when my husband got home from Vietnam, he was very angry at me, too, then thinking this about me, and probably the false pregnancy. However, he never asked me. In twenty years, he never asked me that until the day he called me!

Why do men not communicate? This could have saved our marriage! There was no need to treat me the way he did. I was faithful. He also said his job ended and he had no income. I said, "What about half your inheritance from your mother?"

The sister told him there was nothing left. How on earth was there nothing left? When she moved to Florida, she had $90,000! Well, she bought the sister's house for $37,000, and she was very frugal with money. So the house was then in the mother's name and the sister's name on the deed. Plus, the money in the bank was now in the sister's name. I never thought that my ex should be getting that house since she already got paid for it!

Next we heard he checked himself into a mental hospital because he was suicidal. He called to say he wanted to see the kids. The oldest could drive there. She was eighteen but also worked and went to college.

I took the youngest to see him the next Saturday. He didn't want to see me. I took her on Sunday. She came out and said, "Dad wants to see you." I went in, and he looked drawn and tired. He told me they had him on meds, and he didn't know what was real and what wasn't. He realized that our divorce was his fault, and he took everything out on me and was sorry. Then he proceeded to say that half his pension money went to the girls and half to me. I was shocked at that.

I said, "Don't worry about that now. We need to get you well and in a VA Hospital." He signed a release form for me to have access to his information. We hugged each other and cried. I thought maybe there was hope for him! However, I didn't want to deal with his major depression. We told him we'd be back tomorrow at six for the visiting hours. He said okay.

We went home and told my mother. She was concerned too. We had dinner, and the three of us prayed the Rosary. That night,

I went to the singles dance and told my girlfriends. I just needed to talk to someone who wasn't emotionally involved.

The next day at work, I was thinking about what we had discussed. I called the hospital and wanted to talk to the psychiatrist. He was talking to me about his pension and wanted me to know about it. I felt he had some intentions. I called the hospital four times that day, and he never got back to me. I told them it was important and that I had to talk with the doctor. Nope, no return call.

I went to the chiropractor after and got a phone call from the hospital that they took my ex to the hospital. I asked why. I had to remind them he signed the release papers. She told me he hung himself in the bathroom with his belt! Who gives a suicidal person a belt to wear? I called a girlfriend to pick up the younger daughter and bring her to the chiropractor. The hospital was only one block away. I told her, "Your dad always did things thoroughly, and this doesn't sound good. We got there the same time he arrived by ambulance. He was white as a sheet but breathing. They put him in a room, and I saw him, unresponsive but breathing. I spoke in his ear that he'd be okay and to fight for it.

I saw a tear come down his eye. I just knew he heard me. The nurse said no, it's an autoresponse. He never did that again. I called my sister-in-law to tell her about her brother. Her answer was, "Well, you were always asking him for money."

I said, "Only to help run the household!"

I called my ex-girlfriend as she and her husband didn't know how to manage being friends with me too. I was out of the picture. We'd been friends since the seventh grade! They came to the hospital. We met her in the hall, and my youngest was with me. She came walking down the hall, saying that this was horrible and the next breath saying I was always asking for money. My daughter wanted to deck her. I told her to calm down. To this day, she wished she had decked her. We waited impatiently to find out what the neurologist had to say. We all (family) got called into a room with the neurologist. She said since his brain was deprived of oxygen for too long, he was brain dead. The shock was unbearable as we were going to see him at six, and it wasn't even six yet.

They wanted to know if we would consider organ donation and left us alone. I had no say since we weren't married anymore. The oldest daughter, thankfully, was eighteen and could make decisions. The youngest was fourteen. So we talked. The girls liked the idea their dad would live on in someone else. They agreed. They took him up to a room and had to hydrate him for harvesting the organs. He was on a ventilator to breathe. There was a list of possible things they could use—heart, kidneys, eyes. They ruled out the lungs as he was out of oxygen too long, and they didn't want to risk it. Tissues, ligaments, and skin grossed the kids out. He looked so healthy and pink, hydrated and oxygenated. Now if he could only wake up, which he couldn't. They would wait a few days, and on Thursday, they'd harvest the organs and got ready for the transplants.

I talked with the psychiatrist, and he said, "You told me he wouldn't commit suicide."

I said, "You're the doctor, not me. I hadn't lived with the man for eight years! The man I knew would never do this." He was on suicide watch; every fifteen minutes, he was checked. But he managed to do it in between. I said, "Why did he have a belt on? Every soldier knows how to kill themselves if they're captured."

He said he'd never heard of that.

I said, "I thought that was common knowledge." I said, "Why did you never call me back?"

He supposedly didn't get the four messages to call me.

On Tuesday, when we went to the hospital, my sister-in-law was outside with my ex's boss and my ex's girlfriend. I was thinking, *What a setup this is. Why didn't he call us with condolences first? It was their father. These people are acting like it was my fault he did this.*

When we were in the hospital room with him, there were two ladybugs crawling on the window. This was the middle of the winter. There are no ladybugs in New Jersey now! I told the girls, "One ladybug for each of you from your dad. He loved to garden and loved ladybugs." Somehow, they were comforted.

I had gone to the hospital by myself on Wednesday afternoon. When I was with him alone, his body smelled like it did when he'd come home from work, sweaty. I cried and told him so. Somehow, I felt in my heart he heard me. His best friend came in, and we talked. He asked why I didn't call him. I said, "He didn't want anyone to know because he was embarrassed."

He said maybe he could have helped him.

I said, "He knew we were coming at six, and he did it at 4:45 p.m. He just wasn't thinking right with all the meds." I told him what he'd told me at the mental hospital when we talked. If he'd only gotten help about Vietnam. He just didn't want it; he wanted to forget it. Well, that doesn't work. It just lays dormant and rears its ugly head later. I also told him about the apology, it being his fault, and for taking everything out on me. He said nothing.

His sister stayed at his apartment with the girlfriend who apparently lived with him. They started giving away his stuff. Who were they to do that? The super wouldn't let us in because she lived there. However, he had the lease.

We went to the hospital on Thursday before they took him into surgery. We said our goodbyes. Even the ladybugs had left, and they took him to surgery. It was very sad. We made arrangements at the funeral home for him to be laid out and then cremated. I was able to get him a Mass at our Catholic church since he was still registered there.

Sunday was the wake. We only did one to four; that was all we could take. My family was there. We never saw them, except for funerals and weddings. It was comforting they were there as it seemed to be very strange. My sister-in-law, my cousin, his girlfriend, and my ex-best friend were cooking up something—the four of them hung out together. If I walked into a room they were in, they'd clam up. I was very upset. I felt nervous and shaky. Some of his friends that I knew wouldn't greet me. I felt like shouting, "I didn't cause him to kill himself, what's with some of you?"

I saw a friendly face, his childhood friend and former boss. He gave me a big hug and a kiss. I knew his younger brother and sister more than him.

His girlfriend said she wouldn't be at the funeral. She couldn't take it. So much for love and devotion. I was one of the last to say goodbye. Actually, next to last as my ex-girlfriend and her husband were my ex's best friend and said goodbye last. Whatever. She worshipped him and said he was like a brother. He told her he loved his sister and mother. Boy, what a snow job she got. He couldn't stand either one, but it was the only family he had besides us. The day he put his mother on the plane to move to Florida was one of the best days of his life. We went out to celebrate by eating out. But she was in love with him before I was. She ogled him at the eighth-grade dance. I said, "He was too young for you anyway." Little did we know I'd marry him.

At the funeral, my sister-in-law was nowhere to be found. Really, her only brother's funeral, and she wasn't there? We had the last goodbye, and off to the church service. I was glad the priest allowed it as suicide it was frowned upon by the church. We'd been members since 1975 and baptized and confirmed both our girls there.

The following Tuesday, I went to work. As I went about my typing at work, I was talking to the psychologist who came to test people as to what they were capable of doing, like I got when I was a consumer. I had seen a penny on the floor of my cubie, tails up. I figured I'd turn it over and pick it up when I'd put the mail through the mail machine. Talking to the doctor, I mailed the envelope and came back to my cubical. I sat down and saw the penny was heads up now. I said, "How can that be? It was just tails before I got up to go mail the letter!" I thought about my ex. *Okay, I know you are here.* When we got together with my cousins, we would talk about the afterlife. We'd always said we'd let each other know we were there somehow. Well, he sure did. That penny didn't turn itself over, and no one was in my cubie as I was right by it.

My mom wasn't doing good through all this. First my brother, now my ex, plus losing my father fourteen years before this. It was too much for her. She started having memory loss. She called me at work and said, "I took some meds, but I don't know what."

I went home and called the doctor. She'd taken my blood pressure meds, instead of her own. He said for her to relax and be quiet.

After getting Mom checked by the same neurologist, she told me Mom had Alzheimer's Disease and Parkinson's Disease. She shook inside but nothing visible outside. My mother was a hardworking woman all her life and surely didn't deserve this, especially being almost blind too. She started to slow down a lot after she couldn't do all her walking and taking care of her house since her eyesight got too poor.

I turned fifty and needed a vacation. At the PWP, they were having a group cruise to the Southern Caribbean out of Puerto Rico. I was so ready to get away. Mom told me to go, and she paid for it. It was $1,300 for seven days. There were only four of us. I stayed with one woman in a cabin, and her friend stayed with a guy who came. Just friends. When we were in Puerto Rico, we saw the Fort. Nearby, there was a Blessed Mother statue. You could throw a coin in and make a wish. My wish was that I'd return with my soul mate to make another wish.

I fell in love with the Caribbean water. The Norwegian cruise ship was wonderful with all the food. We stopped at St. Thomas and swam in Megan's Bay. Went to St. Peter's The Great House; what a spectacular view! Tortola was what an island should be, not very inhabited. I loved Aruba and Curacao.

My youngest daughter was having a really hard time through all this. I took her for counseling and stayed home a lot. Mom decided she needed something to distract her from the loss. She loved to swim. So we got an aboveground pool. Of course, Mom paid for it, including a deck. My two cousins put up a six-foot fence around. It was oval, thirty-two-by-twelve feet. Nice to do some laps, four-feet deep. She was thrilled. We'd go out there and swim at night too. She watched Grandma that summer. We gave her a bell in case she needed us. We'd just get in the pool, and she'd ring that bell. We'd take turns who would go in and see what was wrong if we couldn't figure it out through the dining room window. Once in a while, after dark, we'd slip off our bathing suits and swim. It was so wonderful to swim without clothes on. No one could see us as we'd slip on our suits before getting out.

The summer seemed to pass quickly. My daughter was going back to school, and Mom needed care. I had two girlfriends who were HHA, and they took turns taking care of her while we were at school and work. When I got home, I took care of her. She was incontinent, and I changed her diapers, bathed her, and took care of her needs. I was tired of her being in my bedroom, I had no privacy. My oldest daughter was always in the basement, studying and smoking her cigarettes. She said she'd sleep in the basement and give Grandma her bedroom. So the same people who did the deck built a room in the basement for her and put up studs for the walls. We lengthened the basement windows in case there was a fire and she could get out.

Next, the septic tank was backing up. My cousin who had helped build the fence had a friend with a backhoe and dug up around the holding tank. The stones around the holding tank wore down and were now blocking up the holes. I got bigger stones and got them covered up. For $2,500 later, it was fixed. God, this was enough.

The guy who dug the hole was married. He asked my cousin if I was single. He was interested in me. I said no thank you to that! I said, "Lord, isn't there anyone else for me? The next man had to love to dance and love to travel." I was not sitting home and watching the grass grow again.

Mid-October, I went to a singles dance on a Friday night. I saw this guy out on the dance floor with some nice dance moves. I thought, *That's him, the guy for me.* I just knew he was it. I watched him for two weeks to see if he was a womanizer. I'd learned to judge before leaping.

On Friday, November 7, I went to the singles dance. Sure enough, he was there. I watched him for a while. He wasn't hooked up with anyone. In my heart, I just knew it was him. It was just like one of my favorite songs, "Some Enchanted Evening." You may see a stranger across a crowded room, and somehow you'll know; you'll know even then that somewhere you'll see him again and again. For the next slow dance, I went and asked him to dance. His face lit up like a Christmas tree. He was so shocked I asked him to dance!

We danced the rest of the night together, and at the last dance, he gave me a quick kiss. I said, "Slow down." He asked me to go for coffee, so we went to the diner, a Jersey thing to do. We got a table and talked. He couldn't believe I ordered egg whites and toast. Well, it was 1:00 a.m., and after all that dancing, I was hungry. I learned he was twelve years older than me. He didn't look like it. He had no gray hair. He was married, but his wife was in a nursing home with

MS. He'd been taking care of her for twelve years and had to put her in then. His sons told him to go out and have fun now and enjoy himself. He wasn't out but a few weeks when we met. We talked and talked, and I finally got home at 5:00 a.m., I think. My girls were worried. I told them I was fine.

We had a dinner date for Sunday. I told my girls where we were meeting in public, and I was sure he wasn't a serial killer. I'd call them when we were done. We were both into music, me mostly the '60s, him mostly '50s. That was okay because my hobby was listening to music, and I learned who the artists were. My dad was an avid music person, so I knew his songs, especially watching *Name that Tune* on TV and all the variety shows. Perry Como was one of my favorites.

So I told my daughters I was going to Walmart and checking out music with him. Everything was just fine. We got to Walmart and went to the music section, looking at CDs. Who shows up but both my daughters! I said, "What are you doing here?"

"Oh, we're just checking out some music." They were checking out the man who their mother was interested in!

After Walmart, we went to a diner for coffee and laughed about the kids showing up. I got home at a reasonable time. I had work the next day. He was out on disability as he had a stent put in, in February. He was taking care of his wife, but she was now in a nursing home. He was going to put in for retirement as he'd worked thirty years in GM.

Tuesday, November 11, was Veteran's Day. I had off being a state worker. I decided to take my mother and daughter to the beach for a change of scenery. It was cold already but nice to walk on the sand and breathe in the salty air. My mother really enjoyed the day. My oldest daughter had to work, waitressing. When I got home, I got a phone call from my cousin's wife. She had found him dead in their bed. The coroner was coming, and the police were there to make sure there was no foul play going on. Oh my God, I couldn't believe my ears! He was in his early forties. He was like my rock since my ex died. He was there for me, like a brother.

I went to the house and sat with her and the kids. The kids were young; how terrible for them. This was like a nightmare. They did an autopsy on him, which said his body was like that of a seventy-five-year-old man. He drank and smoked a lot and maybe his diet too. The funeral was that weekend. So very sad.

It was at the funeral I was able to reconnect with my other cousin that helped with the fence. We talked about his daughter's adoption and Christening that I knew nothing about. One day, the kids came back from their father's weekend visit and said they were at the baby's Christening. I said whose? I asked them, "Why wasn't I invited instead of my ex?" I was the cousin, not him. Supposedly, my cousin who was staying with them and her family were supposed to have called me and invited me but called him instead. She had a thing for him long before I knew him and apparently still did.

This explained a lot about the night of the wake for my ex and the secrets and plotting behind my back. My cousin, who was like a sister growing up, and my best friend of almost forty years from grammar school both had a thing for the ex. Then his sister who left him no inheritance and didn't go to the funeral—the three of them were backstabbing me. This explained a lot!

While I was on my cruise, we stopped in St. Thomas. My sister-in-law lived there as her husband's father owned a store there. I called him to see how he was. He told me when she left him, she cleaned out their savings account of $50K and left the island. He didn't know where she was. I told him where the inheritance was and that she didn't come to the funeral because she went to see a lawyer if she was entitled to any money! Money, the root of all evil? No, people are the root of that evil. I later got a letter from the lawyer she saw, asking what I was going to about my girls. I told him I was going to take care of them, they were my children, and it was none of his or her business. Don't get the Jersey girl mad or you'll hear it!

My boyfriend and I saw each other every day. Sounds funny at our age to say "boyfriend." but if I said "guy friend." that would mean just friends. We were more than friends. I invited him over for Thanksgiving dinner. He was going to his sister's house and then coming to ours. I had dinner at 1:00 p.m., so I had the rest of the day to relax. He called at 2:00 p.m. to say his sister's oven wasn't working and that dinner still wasn't ready and he came over to eat.

He said he'd rather be with me anyway. It was just me, the girls, and Grandma. Now him.

Christmas was coming, and he mentioned he wanted a leather jacket with a belt. I went to Wilson's Suede in the mall to get it. He'd seen his wife every day. She wasn't talking anymore and just stared at the TV. His son was having a Christmas party, and I was invited. Wow, this was strange to me. He really wanted me to come, so I went. Guess they wanted to check out this woman he was seeing.

The son had a beautiful house in Freehold. I was welcomed and met the whole family. I loved his sister and sister-in-law. Much better than the two I had. Everyone was nice and friendly, and I felt at home.

For Christmas, he gave me a beautiful oval black onyx ring with diamonds around it. I never had anything like this in my life. It was a wonderful Christmas. His wife had a rally and was wide awake for Christmas, talking and joking—a real gift from God for the family. I'd heard of those happening. On New Year's Eve, he wanted to go to the Moose, of which he was a member. I'd never been on a date for New Year's Eve. I was excited.

One day at work, I was in my cubie and smelled cigarette smoke. *Can't be*, I thought, *this is a smoke-free building*. It got stronger! My coworker smelled it too. We almost started gagging. It was so strong. I then said my cousin's name. "Okay, you can stop now, I know you're here!" Just as quickly as it came out, it stopped. I knew he came to visit me. I missed him so. *Love you, cuz.*

The dreaded February was here. His wife was getting bad. It was a matter of days now. "Okay," I said to myself, "she's going to die on the day my ex committed suicide or the day they harvested his organs." I stayed overnight on the second and would leave for work from there. Sure enough, on February 3, around 7:30 a.m., he got the call she'd passed away on the same day as my ex, only a year later. I was glad I was there for him. He couldn't believe she died. I said, "Really? What did you think was going to happen? If I thought she'd be okay, I would have never dated you. I knew this day would come."

He told his son who lived upstairs. I left for work and said, "Call me if you need to talk." He made the arrangements and wanted me to come to the wake. I said, "Are you kidding? That's really not appropriate." He had to get through that himself.

In March, we really needed a break. My mom had an aide, so we booked a vacation cruise for the Eastern Caribbean, leaving Puerto Rico. We toured the island and went to the fort. There was the Blessed Mother. I thanked her for giving me my soul mate that I came with and made another wish in the fountain. We also went to Tortola, St. Thomas, and swam in Megan's Bay, St. Martin, and Dominica. It was a wonderful romantic cruise. Something I'd dreamed about.

In early April 1998, Mom got sick, and I had to call an ambulance. She felt something was wrong with her heart. We actually said goodbye to each other before the ambulance got to the house. She had an enzyme missing in her heart, now causing congestive heart failure. She was eighty-two. At the hospital, the social worker said she would need twenty-four-hour care. I said I had to work, and the kids had school. He said it was best to put her in a nursing home now that she was in the hospital than if she went home, it would be harder to get her into one.

I hated to do this. She was my mother. However, it was best for her to get the care she needed. She got transferred into the nursing home. I told her she couldn't come back home, and she said she understood. She thrived in the nursing home. She actually went around, cheering other people up. All the clothes she'd saved she now wore in the nursing home, all her color-coordinated clothes—she looked so fashionable. She was actually happy. They even bought her, her own dusting kit as she was wiping the molding around the walls. The nurses just loved her.

We got engaged in September 1998 and married in May 1999. He moved in April 1999. Didn't want to set a bad example for my girls any earlier. Mom was able to attend the wedding, and I was thrilled to buy her an off-white suit. One of the aides brought her, and she even got to dance with her brother. She had a ball. My mother's and father's side came along with my hubby's family and our friends together with coworkers. Pictures that were taken with the disposable cameras had pictures of so many orbs, supposedly ghosts not formed yet. They loved to come to celebrations.

Later in the evening, the orbs started to get smoky. If it would have been later, they might have formed into what I don't know.

There were a hundred guests at the Moose Hall—not a fancy place, but it was nice enough. We got home and counted our money. My husband said, "Well, if this doesn't work out, we can always get a divorce!"

I said, "What? That's a crazy way to think. You just promised God you'd love me till death do us part. Now you're looking for an escape if it gets hard. Really! That's pretty screwed up thinking."

We went on our honeymoon cruise to the Mexican Riviera, Los Angeles, and Las Vegas. The cruise was awesome, and we even went horseback riding. Los Angeles was great, visiting the Grauman's Chinese Theater and the bus tour through Rodeo Drive. On to Las Vegas, and we stayed at the Mirage. We did a lot of gambling at slots and tables. We used to go to Atlantic City, so we were seasoned. I wanted to play craps, and he was showing me how.

We walked the strip in all the heat. While at New York-New York, I told him I needed to play craps. I just had to play craps. I had watched this guy throw the dice, and I knew how I wanted to throw them. So we went to MGM Grand. We went up to the crap table and got my $60 worth of chips. I started by putting $5 on the line and $10 to back it up. I threw the dice. I rolled for an hour and a half. I had beginner's luck. The table was so excited with all the numbers I rolled. The guy next to me was playing $125–$150 each number. I was rolling like crazy.

The pit boss said, "Aren't you getting nervous with all this money?"

I said, "No, it's not my money."

I sevened out. Everyone said pass, and I wound up with the dice again. I rolled another one and a half hours. It was time to cash in. We had to catch a plane. The guy next to me said, "Where are you goin'?"

I said, "I have to catch a plane."

He said, "If you keep playing like this, I can buy one and take you home."

I laughed. I was spent physically. I cashed out with $1,200, and my husband had $2,400. We got lobsters to celebrate and caught our plane. While there, we even went on a prop plane and flew over the Grand Canyon and Hoover Dam. It was wonderful, very noisy, and we had to wear earphones.

We came home to married life. I visited Mom in the nursing home and went to work. Sometimes we'd go to AC and gamble. He did the bills. What a relief to not do them. However, if we charged things, he'd only pay the minimum balance. We got into debt quickly after that. I then found out he only wanted to be my husband and not the kids' stepfather. He had OCD, and if things weren't perfect, he'd be complaining. I said, "Leave them alone, they've been through enough with their dad."

He continued to complain, and they could hear him. We had friends over one day, and he was talking about my oldest daughter who heard him in the basement. The kids tolerated him, to say the least.

The oldest went to get her own apartment on the other side of Jersey to be near school. The younger one was going to college now, too, in south Jersey. We talked about moving into a senior development and selling the house that her father and I had built. She had a fit. She didn't want that. She and my husband went at it. He had a few drinks, and they argued face-to-face. He thought it was disrespectful when she talked back. I said, "It's literally half her house too." I had to break the two apart.

We checked out houses in a nearby senior development and found one. We agreed to sell the house as the kids would get half since it was their right as I had divorced their father. We then moved to the senior development. The house was costing too much then with the pool and electric bill and taxes.

We had so much stuff in that moving van you couldn't have put a piece of paper in it. There were two bedrooms, nice sizes, a living room/dining room combination, and another room in the front by the door. It was nice at first. My daughter went to college and met a local girl, and they traveled together to school.

We continued to argue about stupid stuff. When he didn't like the results, he'd say he was leaving. I had many nights of being upset and calling out of work and taking a sick day. To solve our problems, we'd go to AC to blow off steam and gamble. I never did this in my life but found it to be a lot of fun. However, it was costly as money was tight with all the extra spending.

Mom was doing okay in the nursing home. Her brother wanted to move down to the same senior community we lived in. I had gotten my realtor's license, and we helped him move down to the next block. There was a big problem with my mother's family complaining that he was moving down. There was another brother living about two miles away whom he hadn't seen in many years due to a money dispute. I'm not going to go into the details as this family will always start trouble and invent problems where there are none.

My mother was sitting and got up and fractured her hip. She had osteoporosis, and her bones were very brittle. She was eighty-three now. We were due to go on a cruise at the same time. We left after she went back to the nursing home. I was very upset, but the doctor said, "Go, it sounds like you need a vacation." It was great as we went with two other couples.

Mom started being less aware of things now. When I'd visit her, she looked like she knew me. Yet if I asked her my name, she'd say a sister-in-law's name. She was really not in the world. She could feed herself, but that was about it.

June 2000, and it was her eighty-fifth birthday. I brought her a strawberry shortcake. She was in a room where they were playing '40s and '50s music. She just loved it. She ate a lot of cake. I told her if I thought the whipped cream would get her to eat, I'd have put it on everything. Being on Alzheimer's meds made her lose her appetite. She couldn't afford that, only being four-foot-eleven with a petite frame. She went down to eighty-five pounds.

A few days later, she was nonresponsive to eating. They wanted to put a feeding tube in her. I said, "No, I am not going to prolong her agony just so she won't leave me." She was my best friend. There was only one mother, and I was going to lose her. They must have asked me five times if I wanted the feeding tube. I said no! She died exactly one week after her birthday. The last thing I asked her was, "Mom, how are you doing?"

She said, "I'm doing okay."

One brother who was a big problem when my grandmother died, with the house, had never called to see how she was after my father died nor my brother, and he finally came to see her. However, she died before he got there. I thanked God for that. He had hurt her so much.

The next year, the daughter who lived with us met the love of her life. They were so happy. He came to the house to ask my permission to marry her. Of course, I said yes. My advice was to live with him first before you get married. "Learn from me. You really don't know them until you live with them." I told the other daughter the same thing if she should meet someone.

After she left, we decided to move to another senior community, the one my mother had lived in before she moved in with us. It was cheaper living in a co-op apartment. We owned the apartment, but they owned the land. They did a lot of maintenance on it if there were any problems. We saved a lot of money living there. We had to buy it outright but only had to pay the maintenance every month and utilities. We went on a lot of vacations then; we owned a time-share in Aruba for ten years and loved every minute of it. That's my happy place. We went on lots of cruises and back to Vegas, went to Williams, Arizona, and took the train to the Grand Canyon and saw it on a bus tour. It was just spectacular and massive. I want to see it again, people taking their selfies so close to the edge. It was over four thousand feet down, and they went out to the edge! Yikes!

In August 2005, the youngest daughter got married. We all celebrated in AC in June with a bachelorette party. With our comps, we were able to get rooms for everyone. The girls stayed at Showboat, and we stayed at the Hilton. We had a blast. While at Showboat, I put $20 in a dollar machine and won $1,000. I gave the girls money for breakfast, the bride money for her dress, and split the rest with my hubby.

March 2006, I got up to go to work, and my face felt funny. I couldn't control the left side of my face. It was drooping. I could feel it but couldn't move it. I knew it wasn't a stroke. It was Bell's Palsy on my left side. I couldn't even move my eyebrow. I went to the ER, and they sent me to the neurologist. Sure enough, that's what I had. This was terrible! I had some dizziness too. The doctor said it was caused by a virus hitting the seventh nerve in the brain. I tried to take care of myself and watch my blood pressure so I wouldn't have a stroke, like my Dad, but now God gave me this. I had a hard time chewing food as it would get stuck in my cheek.

My older daughter was dating an ER doctor at this time, and he said, "How do they know it isn't a stroke if they didn't do a CT-Scan?"

So my doctor confirmed yes, I did have a brain, but no, it wasn't a stroke. Hopefully, my facial expression would come back. I was out of work for three months. We had a cruise booked for that September. I needed to be off now. I called the cruise line and told them we couldn't come in September but we could do it now. So the following week, for $845 for two people, we did a cruise out of NYC to the Southern Caribbean. We had a wonderful time. Figuring I wouldn't know anyone there, it would be okay. Wrong! I met a classmate on the cruise with her hubby. Go figure. We also met another couple from New York at a bar, talked, danced, and I'm still in touch with her now.

At this time, my daughter got engaged to this ER doctor. He was just the type she was looking for—ambitious and driven to better himself. I said, "Before you get married, live with him first. You don't know what he's really like until you live with him." She later found out that he was so ambitious he didn't really have time for her, even though they lived together. When he was off and they were together, and he'd get called on his day off, instead of being with her, he chose to go to work for the money.

This turned out to be a constant problem. It was either that or he was studying to be a lawyer online. She called me one day, very upset. She had asked for five minutes of his time, and he was too busy for that. So I said, "Is this the life you want?"

She said, "No! I want what my sister has, a loving companion who is there for me, who's willing to do things with me."

I told her, "Then you know what you have to do then."

She broke it off and left him. He was not the one!

August 2006, our office got moved to another building so our state office could be with other state offices with similar services. We moved in, and one week later, I began to feel sick. I had such pain in my eyes. It was like someone poking needles in it. I found a doctor to go to in Point Pleasant. My pressure was up, and he had to laser my eyes. He gave me some drops too. Then I started to experience nauseous symptoms. I'd go to the breakroom, have tea, and feel fine. I came back to my cubie and started feeling sick. It was taking me so much longer to get my work done.

One day, I was going to go to Staples to get something after work, and my boss told me what to get, and I said, "Okay, so I'll go to Home Depot."

She looked at me. I was talking weird. My eyes hurt all the time. They were so dry. I hated any kind of breeze blowing on it, fan or air. The heater in the car made it worse. It's like they were glued inside. After three weeks, I begged my doctor to please put me on leave as I was sick at work, having problems with breathing like asthma symptoms. He put me out of work. A woman from the state came to check out our office as we filed a complaint with our union. She wasn't in our office long before getting an asthma attack herself. She ordered a mold test be done on the HVAC. It took them until December to get to do the mold test.

Sure enough, there was mold in the vents as the HVAC was not working properly. In the summer, it was 78 percent humidity in the office. I had a tester. A guy would come in and work on the system. I said to him, "Why is it so humid in here?"

He said he was only in there to make sure it was cold, not about the humidity.

I said, "Isn't that what an air-conditioner is supposed to do?" They then put a dehumidifier in the office to shut me up. It needed to be emptied twice a day. The ceiling would be leaking, and the tiles would get wet, and they only changed the tiles. We notified PEOCA. They never came until February to test my cubie. It seems the test showed I also had carbon monoxide in my cubie too. That's why I was getting sick. I finally went back to work on the first of February.

PEOCA came then. I said, "What are you testing it for now? Why didn't you come when I needed you?"

They said there were more important places to go and there were only a few people in the office to cover the state!

No matter what I did, I was suffering in the office. It was too dry for my eyes. Being on the computer all day, staring at it, didn't help. I went to Wills Eye Hospital in Philadelphia, Pennsylvania, and they said they couldn't help with the "Dry Eye Syndrome." There was no cure for me. I tried Restasis. It just hurt worse from the time I put it in. It lasted until the next time. I couldn't do that. The doctor who swore he'd fight the state on this denied he ever said it. He got to further his career instead. I wasn't important.

Finally, the governor offered a buyout and offered an extra $500 a month for one year. I retired in July 2008. I was really too young to retire but had no choice. Between my back problems with 22 percent disability, and now this. What could I do?

September that year, I had a hysterectomy. As I was home in bed, I was waiting for my husband to ask me about breakfast. Nothing. Lunch? Nothing. He never thought about asking me if I wanted something to eat. I was in bed resting, and he didn't even consider asking me. Well, that was a big hint of things to come. He'd make it if I asked him, but he didn't think to ask me!

In December 2008, we went on a cruise. We were by the pool. I went in, and my husband walked over somewhere by the pool without his flip-flops on and slipped on the ceramic floor that they had been mopping. There was a warning sign. Not once did he fall but twice. I was in the pool and heard his head bounce on the ceramic floor. I just thought to myself, *This is not good.*

As I packed that night to go home from the cruise, I noticed that my diamond wasn't in my setting. I had lost my engagement ring diamond. I was so upset. I looked throughout our cabin, looked in every suitcase I packed, except the big one. I was exhausted. I thought if it was in there, I'd find out when I got home. God told me it was in there.

When at home, I got up the next morning and started to go through the suitcase. Piece by piece, I took out my clothes and shook them out. Halfway through, I said, "I haven't found it yet, God."

He said, "It's there."

Finally, as I took out the last garment, there it lay on the bottom of the suitcase. I thanked God it wasn't lost. I only remembered this while going through papers. I found the receipt for when the diamond was reset by the store I had bought it from.

When we were home, he soon started to see red streaks going down the TV and asked if I saw them. I said, "No." Then he thought he saw someone and started with hallucinations. He got a CT scan, and it showed a small stroke but from years ago, not now. These symptoms would come and go over the years with no rhyme or reason.

We had gone to an Elks Convention in Wildwood, New Jersey. It was a grand time, and we had lots of fun going places, eating food at the hotel, and dancing. We all knew each other. There would be a parade for those who participated or could participate. I wasn't a member and wasn't capable of doing the walking with my car accident problems anyway. So I'd watch the parade on the sidelines.

One night, when there was dancing, our friends were dancing and one of our friends collapsed. He was down for the count, out cold. He got immediate attention from people who knew CPR, and an ambulance was there in five minutes. They took him away and reported that he was doing fine. I said to my husband, "He's not fine, he's gone."

He insisted that they said he was okay.

"I'm telling you, he died. They're saying that to keep up morale."

Sure enough, he was gone. That day was a downer for sure. However, I heard him say to me, "Tell my wife I'm fine and don't worry."

"Okay, I'll pass that message on to her." The next time I saw her at the Elks, I told her. She thanked me and knew he was okay and with the Lord.

In July, my daughter-in-law's brothers went boating. They were having a good time in a stream on the boat, docked. These guys were always having fun and drinking. They were on this boat, clowning around, and one brother pushed the other, and he went off the boat, into the water. Not thinking about where they were, instead of just falling in the water, he dove in. Unfortunately, the water wasn't deep, and his head hit the bottom. His brother got him out, and they went to the hospital. It was confirmed that he had a broken neck and was paralyzed from the neck down.

We were all in shock at this tragedy. It was just incomprehensible. He was so full of life and only in his forties. The next weekend, a Saturday morning, I was in bed, praying for him. I believe Jesus can do any miracles. I was praying so hard for him to be healed. I heard his voice just like he was next to me! He said, "I don't have to come back."

I said to him, "Who told you, you don't have to come back?"

He said, "Jesus told me I don't have to come back. I'll be okay."

End of conversation with him. I thought, *Wow, I didn't hear that he died.*

I got a text from my daughter-in-law a little while later that he was alert and recognized everyone. I was thinking, *How can that be? He told me he wasn't coming back.* However, that night, he did die. He was in a coma and came out to see them for the last time. I've heard of a rally, and that was it.

At his funeral, I told my daughter-in-law, his mother, and his father of my conversation with him that morning. It was a comfort to them as they are devout believers in Jesus. Rest in peace, he will! Since then, I had a cousin of mine pass, and she told me to tell her sister that she was fine. However, other people get creeped out or just think I'm crazy. She refused to talk with me again and unfriended me on social media. That's their choice. I just relay the message. I'd probably think they're nuts, too, but I know what I know, and I do my job to tell them, that's it.

In November 2009, my oldest daughter got married. She is a doctor and met her husband at a prison she worked in. He being a corrections officer, they became friends. Her car was acting up, and he said he'd look at it. I said, "So he's interested in you."

She said, "No, Mom, he's only going to look at my car and maybe fix it."

I said to her, "No, a man only offers to look at your car if he's interested in you."

She insisted I was wrong. Well, she took the car to him. He fixed it and asked her out to lunch. The rest is history. At first, God gave her what she thought she wanted, then God gave her what she needed.

She didn't want me to walk her down the aisle as my other daughter wanted. When she was eighteen, she thought about finding her birth mother. I was all for it. Who wouldn't want to know? She didn't know I knew her birth mother's name as I had seen it on some papers we signed. They forgot to block her name out. I knew someday, she'd be looking for her, and I'd give it to her, but I'd wait until she was mature enough to handle it. She talked about it when she was twenty-one. I figured she was mature enough then. I gave the information to her. She wasn't ready herself to look.

When she was twenty-five, she decided to go on adoption.com. She saw a woman who was looking for her with the same information as hers and just couldn't respond yet. She got the courage with my encouragement and contacted her. She met her at a diner. She came from a large family and had two half-sisters. Her brother actually owned a condo right below where my daughter lived! Her roots were close by. She eventually met her family. Her grandmother was so happy to meet her, and she saw that she was well taken care of. She and her husband already had so many kids and weren't ready to raise grandchildren. They encouraged the adoption process. She was so very happy it all worked out as she always wondered if they'd made the right decision.

My other daughter and I eventually met her mother, grandmother, and aunts one afternoon at one of the aunts' houses. It was quite a memorable day. My daughter went on to meet many more relatives. We met again at her wedding. She later found out that she had a half-brother who was twenty years younger than her.

After I retired, I wanted to concentrate on deepening my faith and learning how to have some success with praying. I kept watching the ministers or pastors on TV. I learned so much from them. I was never told to read the Bible in the Catholic Church. So I started learning scriptures that helped fit into my life from what was said on TV. I always felt God wanted me closer to him, but with my busy life of working, raising my daughters, and being both mother and father, plus trying to find *me* and more or less trying to find another mate suited for me, I was pretty busy. I was out to live.

After I married my husband, I was content with him. He was my soul mate, but the petty arguing was getting too much. And this 24/7 retirement at my age was rough for me. We did go out and have fun, traveled, gambled, danced, and socialized; but being centered in God was really lacking. I needed peace and somehow didn't have it. My husband was declining, and I saw it. He was twelve years older than me, but ever since that fall, things were different.

In June 2010, I was sitting on my couch with my eyes closed. It was quiet in the condo. My husband was out. As I was there, resting, I got a vision of my daughter holding a little girl's hand and looking down at the ground. I got this feeling it was a graveyard. It scared me as I was thinking, *Was it my grave? Was it where I was going to be, next to my mother?* Well, no, there were no monuments there, but somehow I knew it was a graveyard. I was thinking, *What does this mean now?* My daughter and her husband lived in North Carolina now so she could go to school there. She was in graduate school.

Well, two weeks later, she called me to say she was pregnant! She was taking the pill and had a sinus infection and didn't realize the antibiotics stopped the pill from working, and she got pregnant. She was going to do her internship in the spring of next year but was still in school. She was due in March. OMG! I was so excited to be a grandmother. I just couldn't believe it. I told her, "Well, it's going to be a girl. I saw her with her long blonde hair."

She said, "Oh Mom!"

A few weeks later, I had another vision of a word—*Thea*. Now I couldn't imagine what that meant. Maybe my oldest daughter would adopt a baby with that name? She said she never wanted to have a baby but would adopt. *Hmm, I wonder what that meant?*

January, my daughter, and her husband came up for a surprise baby shower. It was a grand time for sure. My son-in-law, the next month, had the opportunity to go for an engineer's training as he was a conductor. However, he'd have to leave her for his schooling. It was a great opportunity for him to advance. His parents were both sickly at this time. He left for school. She soon would be out on maternity leave from school.

He got notice that his mom had passed. Being nine months pregnant, my daughter was told to stay home by the doctors. She went anyway by train to New Jersey for the funeral. She wasn't going to let anything stop her from being by her husband's side. She then had to go home and be alone now. His school wasn't over. He told her, "Ask your mom to come and stay with you while I go to school."

So I asked my husband what he thought. He was a big family man. He said, "If they need you, then go."

I took the train with her back to NC.

My son-in-law was home in time for the baby to be born. His sister came and was there too. We picked her up from the airport and went out to lunch. We ordered lunch, and my daughter got a migraine. If she got one of those, she had to go to the hospital immediately as her blood pressure would be going up then too. We had food to go and went back to the house. My son-in-law came home from work, and they called the doctor, and off to the hospital they went. His sister and I went too. The wait seemed endless. It was the first baby, and they weren't in any hurry, notably. We got to see her. She said to me, "I don't know how you did it, Mom, not having an epidural shot."

I said, "It was different then. Progress has made it with fewer side effects. You do what you have to do. Take your shots, don't suffer. It eased the pain but didn't stop it."

It was getting late, and we needed to let the dogs out and get some rest, so his sister and I went back to the house. I wanted to take a shower. I tried the bathroom door. It was locked. Don't know how that happened, but I needed a shower. We decided to take off the door. Thank God the hinges were on the outside of the door. We finally found a hammer and screwdriver and got the door off. We laughed! I never told them until recently what we had to do.

Our little girl was born the next day at 4:35 p.m. It seemed like an eternity. She was finally here! My son-in-law came out, beaming, announcing her birth. We all went out to eat as a few friends from New Jersey were there to share the joy with us. I sent my winter clothes home with her girlfriend. The weather was warmer there in March in North Carolina. The baby was home for about ten days, and I decided to go home as her husband had a regular schedule now. I got an airplane ticket to return when I wanted to. I felt like I was abandoning her, but she said to go.

My husband picked me up at the airport. It was great seeing him again. We were arguing on the phone a lot, but it was good to be in his arms and home again if only for a week. We had a special time together, enjoying each other's company. Then it was time to go back to help them out again as my daughter had to go back to school and finish up. She had to graduate in June.

I was enjoying my granddaughter so much. Such a tiny thing. I had forgotten how little babies were. I had sent down a box of my girls' clothes I had saved in my mother's cedar chest. I washed up some of them and took pictures of her in some of them. It was so wonderful for me to do that. I would talk to her and repeat the vowel sounds to her and tell her she was such a good girl. I swore I could hear her mimic "a good" in her throat. No one else got to hear it but me, of course.

We heard on the TV that there was a tornado warning. My daughter was getting almost panicky. I said, "Don't worry, it will be okay. God will protect us. Psalm 91." It was one of my favorite psalms. We were supposed to go to an area where there were no windows. Well, the only thing they had was this closet that was literally two by four feet wide. We had to go in there with the baby. They had stored the bags of large dog food in there. I had to drag these bags of dog food out of this closet. They were huge. I got them and some clothes out, and the three of us went into the closet. My daughter asked how I could be so calm.

I said, "I'm not worried. God will take care of us and protect us."

For a while, we were in this closet and then got the all-clear. The tornado hit five miles away from their house. No matter what's going on around you, God will protect you. Just believe.

Time seemed to go slowly, but graduation finally came. The ceremony was wonderful, and we were so proud of her in her doctorial robe. What a triumphant moment in time! Luckily, I didn't have to walk far or go up any stairs. I just couldn't do it with my back problems. I couldn't attend my other daughter's doctoral ceremony as it was outside and a lot of walking to do. I did get to see it on TV and recorded it on VHS tape. This celebration was in the science museum. We had been there before on other trips. Happiness was in the air.

It was good to get home to my life, and I'm sure my daughter and her hubby were happy to be alone at last. My husband was so happy to have me home. We settled into our life by dancing on the weekends at the clubs he belonged to. I even got him up to sing karaoke after he had a few drinks. He liked to sing Dean Martin and, on rare occasions, he'd sing Al Jolson. He was really good at singing Al Jolson, especially with the encouragement of a bit more alcohol. This was our Saturday nights.

Friday night, we'd go out to eat at one of the clubs for their dinner specials. It was nice. However, as time went on, my husband would get meaner and argue about things on the way home. He would pick a fight over the most ridiculous things, such as I'm driving too slow, why am I in this lane, or to pass some guy up. If I said it was a beautiful night, he'd say something to the contrary. It was a no-win situation. We'd get home, and he'd say he was going to pack up and leave. Always that threat. I'd already been through a divorce, and I wasn't going that route again. It would blow over, and the next day, he'd be nice, like nothing ever happened. However, I was a wreck with the thought of divorce.

We talked less, and when we did, it would lead to some kind of argument. Or he'd say, "Why didn't you say it this way instead?"

I'd say, "It means the same thing."

We'd go around and around, and it got to the point of "Why talk at all?" So I'd talk less to him as it was like talking to the wall. I just didn't understand what was going on here.

When my granddaughter was two years old, I decided I'd like to go to see them for Thanksgiving. My husband agreed, and I went by train out of Trenton. I drove to the station and parked the car. The train ride was endless, it seemed. It was nine hours of looking out the window at the same thing over and over again. It just seemed endless to me. I did bring my laptop and some DVDs to watch. Wi-Fi wasn't that great but was offered. As there were so many people on it, it was hard to get anything. I also brought my MP3 player with lots of music on it. However, I was still restless.

My son-in-law picked me up at the station. What a relief to get off. It was great to see my daughter and granddaughter. She had gotten so big. We had FaceTimed, but it wasn't the same as in person. I went from Wednesday to Sunday. My oldest daughter and her husband and stepdaughter came down on Thanksgiving morning. My son-in-law drove overnight. At last, we were all together again. It was great. I was sad to leave back on the train, but it was as it was—couldn't do anything about that.

On the train ride home, I got a phone call from my neighbor across the driveway. He said my husband was outside with the keys in his hands and didn't know where he was supposed to go. I said for him to call 911 and get an ambulance for him to go to the hospital. I thought maybe he had a stroke. Then I called my girlfriend to go to the hospital and be my eyes for me. I also called one of my stepsons, and he went to the hospital too. When I finally got off the train, I went to the hospital to see what the diagnosis was. My stepson was there and said they didn't find anything wrong. I thought, *And now it begins, the downward spiral.*

I got an appointment with the neurologist for him. Before we went, I wrote the doctor a letter about the things that were going on with him. I didn't want to discuss it in front of him so I wouldn't suffer the repercussions later. This way, the doctor knew ahead of time what was going on. He checked him out and gave him meds for dementia and referred him to get a psychological exam and testing to determine how far things were going. Of course, my husband didn't want to go, but I said, "You're going, that's it!"

Of course, I'd say we'd go out to eat after it, a good incentive to go. The appointment for the testing was in a couple of months. I thought, *God, why did we have to wait so long?* One day, he was talking about killing me! I called the doctor's office, and they got him in for testing right away. He was diagnosed with Mild Cognitive Impairment. They gave him some other meds and told him he could no longer drive a car. To him, this was a death sentence. I knew this day would come eventually and dreaded it.

He'd argue with me that he knew how to drive. I said, "I know that, but now you can't drive." We'd go on and on about this. His stomach would start bothering him again. He'd have bad acid reflux, which he had most of his life. He'd take pills to stop it but then get diarrhea from too much magnesium in the pill. It was a vicious cycle.

One day, I had an appointment with the neurologist and said to my husband, "How about I pick you up for lunch after my appointment?"

He said, "No, not today." Being he was a diabetic, he used insulin to control it.

I got out of my appointment and decided to see if he had changed his mind. He said yes, he'd go. I got home, and he was shaking and said he thought his blood sugar was low. He was shaking and looked pale. I checked his blood, and it was low, in the forties. I gave him orange juice and candy, anything sweet. I called the EMS. They came and checked him. They said to put sugar in the orange juice too. It was going up very slowly. They took him to the hospital, and I followed. He got checked out and was okay. I realized had I not called him and come home, he would have gone into a coma. I was now responsible for the insulin pen. He should have never given it to himself without checking and eating first.

My daughter in North Carolina was a veterinarian. She said, "They give dogs Karo syrup under their tongue to raise the blood sugar. It works really fast."

In 2013, things were out of hand with our finances. We were offered checks to refinance on other charge cards and balance transfers. Finally, we were handling it to the point we could no longer manage it. We talked it over with two stepsons and came to the conclusion to file the awful word: *bankruptcy*. We filed Chapter 13 and had to pay $125 a month for three years. We no longer had our $80,000 debt. It was a relief to not have to juggle the bills to pay all these cards. However, there was no charge card to fall back on in case of an emergency.

So we started to save money, just in case we needed it. We had no choice. We had to remain independent. Luckily, we lived where we did and our living costs were low.

In 2014, we decided on getting a newer car as we were paying on a car now with no warranty. We had to go to the judge and get awarded the okay to finance a car. Since my son-in-law was part owner in a car dealership, we got a newer car at 12 percent on the loan.

In 2016, my husband woke up one day and said to me, "If you want to move to North Carolina, I'll go."

I couldn't believe my ears! I could live by my daughter and her family. This seemed impossible. My daughter was pregnant again and having a boy this time. I was just so excited. Our bankruptcy would be discharged in May. I went online and tried to get a VA loan. Sure enough, we qualified for it as we had faithfully paid on the Chapter 13 debt. My daughter was due in June, so we were planning to go then or after.

We decided to go after the baby arrived. My other daughter went down to watch my granddaughter while she had the baby. I figured there would be enough going on, so we went after that. My grandson was so handsome and little. We scheduled to see some houses. The last house we saw was it. As soon as we pulled into the driveway, we knew this was it. It had the island in the kitchen as I liked and a deck in the back, a vaulted ceiling in the living room to make it feel bigger, fans, and a gas fireplace. It also had a walk-in closet and a soaking tub in the master bathroom. It had a big backyard for the kids to play in—just perfect. The closing date was set for the end of August. We had a lot of work to do. My daughter was elated we were moving by her. We went home to tell the rest of his family.

The boys were not happy their dad was leaving. However, we were doing it. The closing was on my husband's birthday. The kids chipped in and helped us clean out our walk-in attic. It was either yea or nay on the stuff. In one day, it was cleaned out. We got a storage rental and started boxing stuff to take with us. We planned to move on October 1, 2016.

My girlfriend knew of someone who painted, so we hired him to paint our apartment. He used to be a driver for a moving company and offered to drive down a truck. The storage shed was moved by him, and my son-in-law drove the house truck down. October 1, we moved in. It is a very rural town. My son-in-law couldn't believe I moved out in the middle of nowhere. I laughed as it was twenty-five miles away from the state capital. We loved seeing the horses and cows. We claimed them as our own in sight only.

We had family dinners every Sunday at my daughter's house. It was wonderful. Her sister-in-law wanted to move here too. She wanted to retire and live near her brother. Her job called her back, and she went to work. I got to watch my grandson. He was such a doll. He'd come to my house in the mornings my daughter had to work and got picked up later. I worked around their work schedules and took care of my hubby. He didn't require much work yet. He slept a lot. I'd make his breakfast of egg and sausage muffin and coffee and bring it to his bedroom. I'd wake him up to eat, and he'd go back to sleep. The baby had his own little schedule to keep. As he grew older, my husband grew more fragile.

I started to go to caregiver meetings to learn to cope with all of this. Every day, he'd start sundown syndrome around 4:00–5:00 p.m. The belittling and cursing would start. We'd argue about everything and nothing. He would talk filthy disgusting things to me. It was unbearable. I prayed for God to give me strength. It seemed it was around the full moon or new moon he would act up more. I'd call it pre-moon and post-moon syndrome.

I'd take him out to eat, and there would be nothing to talk about or he couldn't hear me, and I'd have to talk too loud for him to hear me. It wasn't worth the conversation. He loved going to Olive Garden, so we went often.

Now he had a hard time keeping his balance. He'd fall a lot. It was embarrassing for him and me to have to be picked up by strangers. We went for physical therapy, but what good would it be if he didn't do it at home? Our granddaughter would get him to do it, but for me? No. He'd just stay in bed too much. I told him, "If you can't walk, I won't be able to take care of you at all."

He developed Parkinson's disease and was shaking quite a bit. The new neurologist said it was part of the deal. He had Lewy Body Dementia, that's why all the sleeping and nastiness. The nurse tried to give him medication for that. He was on it for a couple of days, and one night, we were watching TV. He went into the kitchen and came into the living room. As he walked past me, he ran a knife across my neck. I said, "What the f——k are you doing? You could have cut my jugular vein and killed me!"

He laughed and said he was only joking. Now I thought, *What do I do? Do I call the police or what? If they didn't take him, then it isn't worth it.* I gave him a lecture. He clearly didn't know what he was doing. I locked my door that night and called the nurse in the morning. We stopped those meds.

One night, we both had some wine. He talked some disgusting things to me, saying some stuff I'd never, ever would have done. I then went into the dining room and was drinking my wine, very upset. He came into the kitchen to get a snack. I told him he needed to apologize for what he said. He said he didn't say anything. I said he did. We bantered back and forth. I have a video of the conversations. I could now see he had forgotten what he said in the living room by the time he got to the kitchen. I even made a video to myself of what life was like with him now.

In December 2019, we decided to get our flu shot. Now over the past forty-five years, I had maybe gotten the shot twice. So we went to CVS and got our senior flu shots. Right after that, he kept falling every day. One week later, he told me he had a bad headache. We went to a walk-in clinic to get checked out. I was thinking it was his sinuses as his nose was always dripping. She thought that's what it was. I gave him more aspirin. By 11:00 p.m. that night, he started talking really funny, not getting the words out sometimes. I told him calmly I'd take him to another doctor and get checked out. He went right along with me.

I took him to a local ER. They did a brain scan and discovered he had a brain bleed, probably from falling too much. You don't have to hit your head for your brain to bounce around inside. They took him to the main hospital then. He got in a room and now was not able to walk anymore. He wanted to get out of bed and go home. They sedated him. The meds didn't agree, and he was grabbing things in the air. It was creepy.

A job coach came from the VA. She was a nurse and told me, "Under no circumstances do you take him home."

I told her I knew that from being an HHA. I was not capable of this home care. He needed rehab now. They did it in the hospital. Our insurance company insisted I take him home after two weeks. I said, "No way, I know I can't take care of him." He stayed in the hospital another ten days as the insurance argued I should take him home. I said, "No, he needs rehab."

Finally, he got into a rehab/nursing home. He got the rehab but didn't realize they were holding him up as he was walking. He got angry in the nursing home. There was no phone in the room. He had to go to the nurse's desk to call me. One time, he was by the nurse's station, and the phone rang. He answered it. When it wasn't me, he cursed out the person on the phone. They put him in the dementia ward. He tried to kick down the door. They had to sedate him.

Now he had no bell to call a nurse. He could get out of bed and could transfer to a wheelchair. He was not as bad as other people there. They were in left field. Even I felt creeped out to be there, and so was he. I didn't like the way the nurse treated him and spoke to the director very sternly about his treatment. I got him into a regular room, and he was happier then. He obeyed the rules. I remember once I came to see him, and he saw me down the hall. He gave me the biggest smile. I'd never seen him smile like that. It just warmed my heart.

In February 2020, I learned his sister died. She had cancer. I saw no need for me to tell him of this sad news. What good would it do? I refused to tell him. One of my stepsons argued with me to tell him. He had the right to know. Why? So he could be sad? So it would pull him down? Nope, I was firm on that.

My husband got weaker. He could no longer transfer. It was Valentine's Day. To make it special, I went to the Olive Garden and got his favorite soup and meal. We ate together, and I pulled up our favorite songs that we loved together on YouTube. It was really a soul moment. He couldn't talk, but we just connected on some spiritual level. It was the most wonderful Valentine's Day of our life. I'll never forget it. The tears just rolled down my face as I knew it was our last Valentine's Day together.

He got weaker and couldn't feed himself. I'd go in to feed him. He could say, "Pictures." He wanted some pictures as the walls were bare. I brought one of his lighthouse pictures. It was heart-wrenching to see him like this.

On March 4, I'd been busy going to BJs and the food store to shop. I got a call he was not responsive. I knew this was it. I got in there, and he was hot. I talked to him, and he looked at me. I called a nurse to get his vitals, BP, pulse ox, and temp. The temperature was 101. I don't remember the other vitals. I insisted he have an ambulance. They said they would call a doctor in the morning to see what was wrong.

I said, "Tomorrow? I want to know now."

The EMTs got there and were questioning me if he was always like this.

I said, "No, just take him to the hospital."

They were reluctant.

I said, "I want him taken now! Not wait until the morning!"

They took him.

In the hospital, the triage nurse was excellent. He had two IVs in him and gave him magnesium as he was in pain due to lack of it. He was pulling his knees up in pain. After the IVs, he was awake! I thought, *OMG, he's going to be all right.* I asked him how he was. He said he was fine and asked how I was. I said I was okay.

I told him, "Don't worry, I'm not going to let you be in pain." They gave him morphine. One shot didn't work well enough. They gave him another, then he relaxed and rested. I had the last rites done. The pastor wasn't Catholic or Presbyterian. At this point, I didn't care. "Just pray over him." He did. Then I talked to him.

I thanked him and told him I had seen Jesus and knew he was going to a better place. He was mesmerized by me telling him I saw

Jesus. He asked how and when. He couldn't thank me enough and said it was an honor to meet me. I'm wondering if he was doubting his teaching. Well, that day certainly changed his life too.

My husband stayed overnight and got moved into another room in the ER. That night, I was told he would go into another hospital where they would keep him comfortable as they couldn't do anything more for him. He would be transferred that night for hospice care.

I got to the hospital that Friday. I sat and watch him breathe. His urine was red from not drinking liquids. I could hear his breathing like an echo. I guess that was the death rattle. He was very peaceful and in no pain. I videoed him. Actually, one of his sons wanted to see it. This definitely was the end of my life with him. I was content he wasn't suffering at all. He was peaceful. I sat there and thought, *I just can't watch this hour after hour with no response.* I didn't even know if he knew I was there. I just couldn't sit and watch him breathe. It could be hours, and to be there alone was eternal. I kissed him goodbye and left. I'd be back tomorrow.

I got a call at almost 1:00 a.m. that he had passed at 12:45 a.m. It was over. I thought, *Now what do I do?* I called my daughter, and she said she'd meet me at the funeral home and to just let her know what time. I knew which one I wanted as I had talked with them at a caregiver meeting. It would have cost $10,000 to transport him to New Jersey on a plane and then to another funeral home for a viewing. I spoke to my stepson that morning, and he said, "Don't waste the money, you'll need it for yourself. Have him cremated and bring him." So that's what I did.

My daughter and I went the next morning to make the arrangements. I said I needed to see him. Up to this point, it was all talk. So they arranged for me to see him. They gave me his wedding ring, and I talked to him to say goodbye. He was cold, and I cried. It was twenty years, almost twenty-one. It was a stressful marriage. One day, before he got very sick, he told me I was the love of his life. I was shocked. I said, "Why didn't you act like that? We would have had a better life."

He said he didn't know why. It was over now.

My stepsons arranged a celebration of life get-together at one of their houses. I arranged the burial plot next to his first wife. He was married to her for forty years. It was only right. The pandemic hit. The governor of New Jersey wanted to close the borders. We got up early and left. Certainly, we didn't want to be stuck there for sure.

At first, it was okay. I didn't have to worry about him anymore. After two months, I thought I could do this. Then it hit me that this was it. Nothing was going to change from here. The shock hit me. I started to get sad. Now what was I going to do? With COVID-19, we all had to stay home. Now I was free to live my life, but I had to stay home! Really, God!

Luckily, we continued to have family dinners, and I watched my grandson. He wasn't old enough for school. We had to make do with what was. We got a stimulus check from the president. However, the $1,200 I got for my husband needed to go back as per the *media*! One journalist posted a coffin on the front page, saying that anyone who died that year had to return the check. I sent him a message about how mean and hurtful that coffin was. I didn't need to be reminded my husband was dead. He apologized to me. As a good citizen, I mailed the check to the IRS. Then they decided we didn't have to return it! I requested it on the 2021 tax form and got a letter it was in the mail soon. Yeah, right, I still don't have it.

I was sitting in my chair in the living room and heard my husband's voice say to me, "You were right what you told me about Jesus and heaven. I didn't want to believe you, but you were right."

I was preaching to him all the time to listen. He was getting closer to his time, and he better declare that Jesus was his Lord and Savior so he could go to heaven. I was shocked to hear him and to finally admit it was true. He finally saw for himself.

Another time, I was thinking of him in bed. And he said to me, "I want to you know I'm all right."

I said, "How do I know it's really you?"

He said, "Why didn't you tell me my sister died? She's here with me."

Well then, I knew it was him because I never told him. I said, "You were too sick to get such news like that. You'd find out soon enough."

People find this strange, but I'm sure there are more people out there not letting everyone know it's happened to them too. They can communicate by blinking the lights. My uncle actually shut off the TV when we were at the house, eating. He hated the TV being on and no one watching it. We all looked at each other, and no one touched the remote.

I was restless and lonely. I joined a dating group. One guy asked for my phone number. My cellphone was out of state, so it didn't matter. He was supposed to be in the next town. Well, he called. I checked it out, and his landline was in Connecticut. It got him kicked out. Another guy couldn't get his story straight. He was in the next town too. That got him kicked out. One guy would have been great, but he rode a motorcycle. With these people, the way they drive, there was no way I was going to be on a motorcycle. That ended that.

I was disgusted with dating already. By the end of 2020, I met with a grief share group from the same place as the hospice hospital. We met for ten weeks online. We all lost our spouses. Four women and one man. We are friends to this day. We all understand each other on a very special level.

In the summer of 2021, I told God if I'm meant to be with someone, I want him to be—and I gave God a list. The last two men, I wasn't specific. This time, I was—kind, understanding, etc. And I'm not going to go looking for him. He'll have to call me.

On August 6, 2021, I got this message from my first husband's boss that he wanted to speak to me.

I was thinking, *What on earth does he want to talk to me about? Maybe he's on a fact-finding mission to give my ex-sister-in-law some info or my ex-girlfriend.* I can't remember from the viewing if he was a friend or an enemy. He said the best time to call him was 9:00 a.m. I was thinking, *I'm not up by 9:00 a.m.* I left him a message.

On August 21, I had to babysit the kids, so I was up at 9:00 a.m. I called him. We had a nice talk. He said he was easygoing and gave me a lot of his qualities. After we hung up, I was thinking it sounded like he was giving me a resume or applying for a job. It was weird.

The following Friday, he called and said that I had kissed him at the ex's wake, and he never forgot it. It helped him get through many hard times in the past twenty-four years. I was shocked when I hung up. I kissed him at my ex's wake! I don't remember that. It was a rough night with the backstabbers there. I couldn't remember who was my friend or not. I kissed him like that and said, "Oh. Really!"

Then I was making a sandwich, and the Holy Spirit said to me that he was pure. I was shocked. I could believe him. He told me that he saw Jesus, too, and that he prayed every day when he got home from work. Wow, could I really trust what he's saying to me?

We continued to talk every day. He said that my cousin worked overnight with him, and he gave him my phone number. Now what were the chances my cousin worked at this local store and gave him my number? Did God do this? How else did this happen?

I had sprained my back prior to this phone call and started physical therapy. Then I got an abscess on my abdomen and had to go to the ER. I was in the ER to get this drained, lying on the gurney. I was thinking his full first name was Theodore. Wait, Thea? Theadore is how it's pronounced! OMG, the mystery is solved, it's him God? I got a peaceful warmth going down my body as a sign of yes! I had a high for about an hour and a half after that. It was just indescribable. He was my "Thea" from twelve years ago!

We talked every day, twice a day. We discussed everything—our marriages, politics, current events. We were so much alike and had the same interests. It was like he was my male twin! I decided I just had to go see him. He arranged to take off work. They were shocked as he never took a vacation.

I was sitting on my front porch and was talking to God. I said, "Would you be upset if we had sex?" I asked outright. My answer was a chastity belt. A definite answer of no way to that. Like, what kind of Christian people would we be if we did that? That's for married people only. Since we were followers of Jesus and in his world and not of this world, it was a no-no.

In November, I just had to go see him. The kids were tracked out, and I was free to go. My kids were having a fit. "Mom, you don't know who he is now."

"I know him, I hung out with his brother and sister. He was my ex's childhood friend. I'm not afraid."

They made me promise to rent a car so I would have an escape route, being I was staying at his house. I bought this ticket, rented the car, and nothing was going to stop me. He was my soul mate, a spiritual soul mate. He said he'd give me a check for my expenses, and he did. I had the best time of my life. The best five days of my life. We talked, danced, and went out to eat. We went to see the old neighborhoods, called my girlfriend whom he lived next door to, and called his brothers and sister plus a childhood friend of ours. We went to the beach and had a picture taken of us. I looked ten years younger, my friends told me. He wanted to come and see me for Valentine's Day. It seemed like an eternity away. It was set for February 8, and he'd come.

The holidays came. Just before Christmas, my daughter-in-law's mother got COVID-19. She had COPD and was having a rough time with it, then went to the hospital. It didn't look good. I got a call she passed. I then heard her say, "It's time for me to go. Don't forget to write that book."

Now how did she know I was writing a book? I only told my daughter here, her sister-in-law, and my granddaughter. It was very sad, but we all knew she had gone to be with Jesus, and that was of some comfort. She was very religious and knew she was at peace.

The time got closer for him to come. He seemed to be preoccupied with work. It seems they were looking now to get rid of some overnight employees. They were trying to fire him. They fired my cousin, saying he wasn't working enough. I could tell he was stressing out. He was working harder as they were pressing him harder. He was getting tired. He wanted to work as he had a goal in mind. He was still rehabbing houses and wanted to get ready to sell his house. My cousin's son renovated his both bathrooms and kitchen between Thanksgiving and Christmas. He wasn't getting the right amount of sleep. What was left was the front of the house.

In January, he was stressed out due to work. They were trying to get rid of a lot of overnight workers. He was the oldest. However, he proved he could keep up with all of them. He had a mission, and nothing was going to stop him. He was more tired, I could tell. We were talking every day, sometimes two to three hours a day, then at night, he'd have me on the phone while he went to work. He decided he'd come around Valentine's Day. How romantic, but could he get off work? Now it was uncertain when he would be able to come.

It's certainly up to God where we'll go from here. Everything is in God's timing, not ours. We'll just have to wait and see what he decides.

After reading through all of the things I had been through in my lifetime, even I'm surprised how stressful it's been. God has chosen me to do this. I certainly wasn't qualified to start this, but he kept at me to do this and let the world know about my experiences.

I've learned there are no coincidences in life. It's all God's plan for us. The day I took my mother to see Connie Francis and saw that man pushing his wife in the wheelchair, little did I know he would soon be my husband! He had a car accident just before I met him on November 3. That's the same day I had my car accident only seven years earlier. His wife died on the same day my ex committed suicide only the year after. Everything in my life is within eight days of something else significant. My mother died seven days after her birthday. My brother died seven days before my parents' anniversary. My father died the day before his mother's birthday. I had my daughter eight days before my brother's birthday. My grandson was born eight days after my mother's birthday and the day before she died. My granddaughter was born eight days after her grandfather's birthday, and my second husband died two days before my first husband's birthday and was cremated on his birthday.

My oldest daughter got married on my first husband's and my anniversary. She was born five days before my father's birthday, and my mother's birthday was eight days after my father's. Theodore's birthday is two days after my granddaughter's. I was born at 8:35, which was the year my husband was born. We bought the house on his birthday, and we were born in the same city.

At times when things are happening, it seems so devasting. However, it felt devasting and unbearable every time things went wrong. God has our life planned out. We're here to ride it out the best we can. He doesn't expect perfection only a willingness to follow it through. Just keep on course and live life the way he has it planned. Every day is not a good day, but just stay focused on the day. It will get better as long as you have hope and faith.

I gave no one a name as the glory is to God only. I only mentioned one name to get my point across. Everything I said in *My Walk with God and Beyond* is truly my experience with him and others.

I finished this at 8:35 a.m., the time I was born, and today is my birthday!

ABOUT THE AUTHOR

Bogga, as she is affectionally called by her grandchildren, was born in northern New Jersey. At the age of ten, her family relocated to central New Jersey to improve the family's economic situation. Being the creative type, after graduating high school, she attended Wilfred Beauty Academy and became a hairdresser. She was determined to be independent and make her own way.

When Congress authorized troop deployment to Vietnam, she married her high school sweetheart before he was deployed. Over the years, she worked several jobs, which included managerial positions.

She later remarried and retired. Bogga has two grown daughters, both doctors, and currently resides in North Carolina to be close to her younger daughter and enjoy her grandchildren.